AF540860

URBANISATION AND HEALTH

URBANISATION AND HEALTH

By

Dr. M. Lakshmi Narasaiah
M.A., Ph.D.

Professor of Economics
Co-ordinator, Dept. of M.B.A. and Commerce
Special Officer
Sri Krishnadevaraya University Post-graduate Centre
Kurnool–518 002
Andhra Pradesh
(India)

DISCOVERY PUBLISHING HOUSE PVT. LTD.
NEW DELHI-110 002

First Published-2008

ISBN 978-81-8356-312-3

Published by:

DISCOVERY PUBLISHING HOUSE PVT. LTD.
4831/24, Ansari Road, Prahlad Street,
Darya Ganj, New Delhi-110002 (India)
Phone: 23279245 • Fax: 91-11-23253475
E-mail: dphbooks@rediffmail.com
dphtemp@indiatimes.com
Website: www.discoverypublishinghouse.com

Printed at:
Arora Enterprises
Laxmi Nagar, Delhi–110 092

Preface

Is abandoning the cities the answer to the growing ecological problems of urbanisation? The trend at any rate is in the opposite direction. At the beginning of this century, only every 10th person worldwide was a city dweller. At its end, more than half the global population will be urbanites. And most of the urban population growth will take place in the developing countries, led by Asia.

Compared to other parts of the world, however, the urbanisation process in Asia is currently not even particularly far out in front. Worldwide, city dwellers account for 43 per cent of the total population. Industrial nations have an average urbanisation rate of 72 per cent. Less industrialised countries have 34 per cent. In the Asia-Pacific region the rate is 30 per cent, in Latin America 72 per cent, and in Africa 33 per cent. The urbanisation growth rate in a number of Asian countries has in fact slowed compared with earlier years. Nevertheless, not only industrialisation, but also the increasing degree of urbanisation has emerged as a growing burden on the environment in many Asian countries.

Changed Urbanisation Pattern in India

Environment burdens are just as much a problem in the old industrial nations as they are in India. But each group has a specific pattern of development. The urbanisation process in India has proven to be more pollution-intensive than that in the old industrial nations of Europe and North America. There are several reasons for that:

Dr. M. Lakshmi Narasaiah

Contents

1

Towards Healthy Cities

More than a third of the urban population in developing world live in housing of such poor quality with such inadequate provision for water, sanitation, drainage, garbage collection and health care that their health is constantly under threat. But, properly planned, cities can be safe and healthy.

In the cities of India, it is common for one child in three to die before the age of five and for virtually all infants, children and adults who survive to have disease burdens many times higher than they should.

Diarrhoea, tuberculosis and respiratory infections (each among the largest causes of death) are generally much increased by over-crowding. Many accidental injuries happen when there are three or more persons living in each small room in shelters made of flammable materials and there is little chance of providing occupants (especially children) with protection from open fires or stoves.

But cities also include some of the India's safest and most healthy neighbourhoods. High densities allow much lower costs for supplying each household with piped, treated water supplies and most forms of health, educational and emergency services.

Sanitation and drainage may be costly in cities, as complex systems are needed to cope with high densities and large population concentrations but city households can generally afford to pay more—and are prepared to do so if they get a good service.

Cities may be considered ecologically unsustainable because of high consumption and waste levels but well planned and managed cities can combine high living standards with remarkably low levels of energy consumption, resource use and wastes. The concentration of people and production creates many more possibilities of collecting and recycling wastes and for walking, bicycling and a high quality public transport.

For many, city-life is one of excessive workloads and drudgery, yet cities remain centres of culture—including the visual and decorative arts, music, dance, theatre and literature. Most cities have a large reserve of young people on whose initiative and energy they could draw to improve conditions—yet most such people find that their cities offer them little hope and little prospect of employment. If cities have such potential to provide healthy, stimulating and valued places to live and work for all age groups, why do so few achieve this?

Supporting Change

Much of the explanation is the lack of 'good governance'. Good governance in any city means encouragement and support from all levels of government for a great range of investments of capital, expertise and time by individuals, households, communities, voluntary organisations and NGOs—as well as private enterprises. In most cities in India, the total value of investments made by people in their own homes and neighbourhoods exceeds many times the total value of capital investments made by city and municipal authorities. Yet governments and aid agencies usually ignore (or deem illegal) most such efforts.

Most households who want their own home cannot afford to purchase one—or at least one that is legal. They cannot obtain housing loans so the cost of the house purchase can be spread over a number of years—as they cannot meet the (usually) inappropriate conditions set by banks or housing finance institutions. If they turn to building their own home—as most do—they have to occupy or purchase the site illegally. They often have to build on dangerous sites—in floodplains or on slopes with frequent landslides or mudslides—as the cost of safer sites is too high.

Even if they can qualify, for a housing loan, most such loans are for finished houses, not for incremental construction. And even when they have developed their own home and neighbourhood into a viable residential area, governments usually refuse to provide these with roads, water supplies, drains and other essential infrastructure, because they are 'illegal'.

What would cities look like today if governments had supported these individual and community efforts by ensuring that land, building materials, credit and technical advice were as cheap and readily available as possible? Or if government-community partnerships had been formed to, at least, improve water supply, sanitation, drainage and health care.

These work within what is often called the 'social economy'—the great variety of initiatives and actions that are organised and controlled locally and that are not profit-oriented. The social economy includes the work of citizen groups, residents' associations, street or barrio clubs, youth clubs, and parent associations that support local schools. It includes many voluntary groups that provide services for the elderly, the physically disabled or other individuals in need of social. It often includes many initiatives that make cities safer and more fun-helping provide supervised play space, sport and recreational opportunities for children and youth. It may provide formal or informal supervision or maintenance of parks, squares, and other public spaces.

The social economy not only 'gets things done' but also creates a dense fabric of relationships that allows citizens to work together in identifying and acting on local problems. Its value to a 'healthy city' is enormous, even if it is often forgotten by governments and international agencies.

The capacity of city authorities to govern is not the same as the capacity to invest, since these authorities can do much to encourage and support the social economy. City authorities can often greatly increase the supply and reduce the cost of land for housing by changing inappropriate regulations, streamlining planning and land use control, procedure and making better use of publicly owned land.

City authorities should also have the main role in enforcing legislation on, air and water pollution and occupational health and safety. This does not require large investments by public authorities, but it can do much to improve health and the quality of life in a city. Good governance also means managing competing claims and finding common ground between enterprises, trade unions and residents about what should be done to make the city more healthy.

Achieving a healthy city needs a representative political system through which the priorities of citizens and businesses can influence policies and actions. Democratic structures remain among the best checks on the misallocation of resources by city and municipal governments. Actively involving a wide range of local groups in developing 'city governance' helps ensure that the different priorities of a wide range of groups are addressed.

The key issue is not so much identifying what should be done to achieve more healthy cities. This is well-known. It is identifying how it should be done, especially how governments and international agencies can support a vast range of activities by individuals, households and communities that help build and maintain healthy cities—which to date they have ignored or even (for many governments) repressed.

****

2

Urbanisation and the Environment

Is abandoning the cities the answer to the growing ecological problems of urbanisation? The trend at any rate is in the opposite direction. At the beginning of this century, only every 10th person worldwide was a city dweller. At its end, more than half the global population will be urbanites. And most of the urban population growth will take place in the developing countries, led by Asia.

Compared to other parts of the world, however, the urbanisation process in Asia is currently not even particularly far out in front. Worldwide, city dwellers account for 43 per cent of the total population. Industrial nations have an average urbanisation rate of 72 per cent. Less industrialised countries have 34 per cent. In the Asia-Pacific region the rate is 30 per cent, in Latin America 72 per cent, and in Africa 33 per cent. The urbanisation growth rate in a number of Asian countries has in fact slowed compared with earlier years. Nevertheless, not only industrialisation, but also the increasing degree of urbanisation has emerged as a growing burden on the environment in many Asian countries.

Changed Urbanisation Pattern in India

Environment burdens are just as much a problem in the old industrial nations as they are in India. But each group has a specific pattern of development. The urbanisation process in India has proven to be more pollution-intensive than that in the old industrial nations of Europe and North America. There are several reasons for that:

- industrialisation in India is restricted to a few locations which are often concentrated in and around capital cities. Although environmental damage continues to be minor at a national level, these locations have higher pollution levels than those ever reached in industrial nations;
- furthermore, besides the strong regionalisation of industries, the industrialisation pattern of India shows a great diversity of environmental hazards. The trend to establish "last industries first", which is promoted by progressive industrialisation, leads to a country producing certain dangerous materials before they have been covered by state regulations;
- the time factor has to be seen as an important element in the emergence of these already highly regionalised environmental burdens. In India industrialisation and its concomitant urbanisation is taking place within a ban population grew tremendously.

Growing Environmental Damage

Water pollution in India is caused mainly by domestic sewage. For example, households are responsible for 75 per cent of the pollution of the rivers. The domestic sewage problem got more and more out of control with growing urban populations. Pipe-based waste water systems are rare in this country. In India dealing with waste has an extremely low priority. The type of waste disposal depends mostly on what the cities can afford. The present level of air pollution is also very high.

Innovative Approaches to Solutions

Environmental protection and economic development are seen as contradictions. Economic development can only be achieved at the cost of higher levels of environmental pollution. And in reverse, if pollution is to be controlled and reduced this can only be done to the disadvantage of further development. In the meantime, however, numerous instances of successful urban environmental management are developing. They could help to change and subsequently breakthrough the existing pattern of thinking. The following approaches can be viewed as important.

Combining regulations with incentives: The introduction of lead-free petrol and the mandatory equipping of new cars with catalytic converters is still by no means common in India. As numerous cars without catalytic converters are still able to use lead-free. Converters were then at first made compulsory for higher-powered cars, and later also for compact models.

Combining regulations with simple controls: Apart from general limitation of the number of cars in the city, its most important single measure to prevent traffic jams and the additional petrol consumption and pollutant emissions caused by them.

High economic growth in India has in fact led to a general reduction of poverty. But the distribution of income, particularly between urban and rural areas, has remained relatively constant. Urban environmental and traffic problems have increased heavily during the same period. These developments can be attributed to a certain pattern of official action (or "non-action"):

- governments have made efforts in supplying roads, but neglected the demand for mobility;
- governments are preoccupied with supplying water, and have neglected follow up problems, above all the questions of waste water disposal and treatment. In Indian cities, for example, this leads to the absurd situation that due to the mushroom like growth of the cities and the increased water pollution linked with it, water must be brought in over ever greater distances and at ever greater expense;
- governments take a one-sided look at noxious substances. Concentrations of harmful substances in water and in the air are in fact checked, and some measures are taken

against individual pollutants of single sectors (e.g. lead emissions by the transport sector).

But an integrated policy which operates integrated environmental management with the aim of comprehensively relieving the burdens on the environment has not yet been developed anywhere. To consider such a concept, it is necessary to cut loose from the customary way of approaching problems. It makes sense not to separate the problem areas from each other according to sectors and pollutants, but rather on the basis of their ecological impact.

Orienting on demand hits the core of the concept of ecological modernisation, which is about reducing the intensity of resource use (note, at this stage this does not yet mean the absolute reduction of inputs). At the same time, sights are set on a lower use of land with the same size of population, or also lower energy consumption with the same degree of added value or the same per capita income.

Finally, the importance of governments for creating framework conditions must be emphasised once again. Because the actors come from different spheres, such conditions are essential.

From the time of the Greek polis, it was the ambition of the Greek city councillors to pass on a city that was more beautiful than the one they had taken over. There is a long way to go before such an attribute asserts itself in India (and elsewhere).

****

3

Urbanisation in India and Limitations

Urban growth is an undeniable fact of the future in India. Only 1 in 10 people lived in cities when this century began; nearly half will by the century's end. Urban migration accounts for a large share of this rapid growth. Upto 60 per cent of the people in many cities in India live in burgeoning, impoverished squatter settlements.

Allowing urban development to spread out upon undisturbed land exacerbates automobile dependence and destroys the natural environment. Yet it is impossible to truly halt development; prohibiting growth in one jurisdiction merely shifts it to neighbouring areas. The key to a livable and viable future for the India's urban areas is neither to encourage sprawled growth nor to try to stifle growth altogether—but rather, to encourage compact growth.

Forward-looking Municipalities have discovered that compact development can accommodate expanding populations without despoiling the surrounding environment. These cities are actually using urban growth to their advantage: for example, compact development, by making public transit, cycling, and walking more practical, reduces reliance on cars so that less energy is used and less pollution generated. Filling in their under-used space has allowed these cities to become more pleasant and convenient places to live. With less space paved over for parking lots and urban highways, more room is available for homes, workplaces, and green space.

In the long run, population stabilisation—via more effective family planning and elimination of poverty—is essential to the future of the Indian cities. But it will take decades to stabilise population growth. In the mean time it is essential for urban areas to begin redesigning themselves. With compact development, urban areas can meet people's expanding needs by making the most of existing space.

Somewhere to Grow

Many cities have so much underused space that they could develop for decades to come without bulldozing another square yard of undisturbed land. Although much underuse of property results from individuals and companies holding it for speculation, local governments themselves frequently hold large amounts of vacant real estate. Surplus government buildings and other public holdings often stay idle while growth mushrooms a the city's edge. In India great potential for filling in underused space lies in redistributing urban land ownership. Land reform, granted, is among the most difficult political moves a government can undertake. Yet the need for such an effort is difficult to deny.

Cities have tremendous scope for making urban growth more compact by establishing urban growth boundaries outside of which further development is prohibited. Greenbelts surrounding cities perform this function in India. Cities of strict landuse planning charge that urban growth boundaries and other bold measures encroach on individual freedoms. Yet guiding development more rationally can in fact do more to protect people's rights, while keeping cities livable.

Urban Density: The Real Story

Often, people move out to the suburbs seeking open space and bonds with nature that come only in a rural setting. Yet most of these residents continue to maintain an urban life style—commuting to jobs in the city and demanding an assortment of urban amenities found in suburban shopping malls. The result is neither urban nor rural living, but a destructive compromise that the environment cannot sustain.

The low-density suburban model not only has come at a high ecological price, but it also has failed to deliver on many of its promises. Seeking freedom, mobility, fresh air, and access to open space, many suburbanites instead encounter long commutes and traffic jams caused by the dispersed communities' nearly exclusive reliance on private automobiles. Suburban life promises escape from crime in the city, only to trade that danger for the far greater chance of being injured or killed in a car accident. And a new form of social inequity has emerged, stranding anyone who cannot drive or afford a car.

Although denser landuse could help solve the environmental, social and aesthetic problems of sprawl, widespread misconceptions about increased density—even moderate density—often prevent communities from adopting compact landuse strategies. Contrary to popular belief, augmenting the density of development does not create a harsh physical environment. Planners and citizens, often assume that moderate and high-density landuse are synonymous with crime, poverty and squalor. Yet there is no scientific evidence to support a direct link between these social problems and density.

Transport's Missing Link

One of the most destructive by products of low-density sprawl is an automobile-dependent transport system. The pattern of urban development dictates whether people can walk or cycle to work or whether they need to travel dozens of miles; it also determines whether a new bus or rail line can attract enough riders. Despite this obvious link, city layouts often are too dispersed to foster efficient transportation. Many of the India's cities have failed to implement compact land use as a transport strategy; few foresaw that an automobile orientation would later plague them with traffic jams, deadly accidents, harmful noise and smog, while marginalising people who do not own cars. A more rational approach for Indian cities would be to integrate homes not only with workplaces but with commercial, recreational and other land uses so they are easily accessible without cars. Such reforms ideally would not hamper developers or impose uniformity, but instead would lift restriction that create unnaturally one-dimensional districts.

The key to making integrated zoning work well as a transport strategy is to encourage urban development that is dense enough to promote alternatives to cars. For example, transport planners estimate that an Indian city typically requires at least seven dwellings per acre in a given area to support reasonably frequent local bus service, nine dwellings for light rail and 15 dwellings for an express bus. These moderate densities can be reached by mingling clusters of single-family homes with garden apartments and two-to six-story apartment buildings.

Many large cities are finding that the most transport-efficient land use pattern combines a compact, well-mixed downtown with several outlying, high-density areas—all linked by an extensive public transport system. This way, people can walk, cycle and take short public transport trips within a given area and reach other areas via express bus or rapid light rail.

Room Enough for All

Attempts to slow or stop growth shut out many groups of people—and by restricting the supply of housing, tend to inflate home prices. Compact growth, by contrast, can help create diverse communities and promote smaller, more affordable housing.

Cities of India can combine compact growth with strategies to increase the supply of land available for low and moderate-income homes. India can made use of measures to prevent speculation, a process whereby land owners in nearly all free-market societies hold land as an investment for future windfall gains, rather than putting it to current use. Speculation puts upward pressure on real estate prices and idles great amounts of urban land.

By taxing vacant land according to its true worth in the market, cities can make these parcels less attractive as an investment vehicle. Local governments typically assess such properties at far less than their market value, effectively rewarding property owners for keeping their land idle. More accurate property assessment encourages redevelopment. Cities can go a step further to tax vacant land more heavily than developed parcels. To avoid spurts of sprawled growth, however, it is critically important to combine these tax strategies with clearly defined growth frontiers—such as greenbelts and urban growth boundaries—that contain development within the existing urban area.

Municipalities can enhance the supply of affordable housing require each house to occupy its own spacious lot with controls that promote a variety of housing types, including smaller and multi-family homes.

A more immediate remedy to the housing crunch felt in many cities, where homes tend to be large, is to allow single-family home owners to rent out small apartments within their homes. The size of the average household is shrinking steadily as couples have fewer children and more people choose living arrangements other than the nuclear family. As a result, many homes built for larger households can create an extra unit in a converted basement, garage, attic or even an added story.

Laying the Groundwork

Creating compact cities requires a commitment by planning authorities and governments at the local, regional and national levels. Adequate local planning institutions are especially lacking in the developing world. Municipal government in India often have neither the authority to guide land use nor the funds to provide basic services. With few exceptions, urban planning is a relatively recent phenomenon in India.

Compact growth of cities also hinges on regional cooperation, an important tool for handling conflicts between the interests of individual localities and those of the broader region. All cities in India are required to plan their own development according to stipulated goals, such as energy conservation, protection of open space and provision of affordable housing. These statewide planning requirements not only enhance regional cooperation, but they also give cities the backing they need to apply a comprehensive, long-term vision to their landuse planning.

Finally, the effectiveness of urban planning can be fully achieved only if governments remove the conflicting incentives posed by other national policies. Among the greatest barriers to compact urban development are artificially low petrol prices, which encourage dependence on cars.

If the barriers to efficient landuse were removed, what would a compact city look like? Much of the vast space normally devoted to automobile parking in a sprawled, car-dependent city would be planted in trees and flowers, or used for building homes. Old properties would be revived for new uses; a 19th century warehouse into apartments, a vacant lot into a public park, for instance, the downtown area would be lived in day and night, with apartments and offices occupying the floors above ground-level shops. Each district would be home to a variety of jobs, shops and day care centres, all within an easy walk or bicycle ride. People could travel quickly to other parts of the city and outlying areas via rapid rail and express bus lines.

On a rapidly urbanising India, societies can take greater command of their fate by more consciously determining the use of urban land. Whether surrounded by affluent suburbs or makeshift shantytowns, the cities can protect the environment and better address the needs of current and future generations by planning for compact growth.

* * * *

4

Cities Residents to the Rescue

In the next ten years, the number of people living in cities will rise to around 3.3 billion. Tokyo already has a population of 27 million, Sao Paulo (Brazil) 16.4 million, and Mumbai 15 million. World Bank forecasts show as much as 80 per cent of the developing countries economic growth occurring in the cities and major conurbations.

There are both positive and negative aspects to these developments. At each stage in the history of urbanisation, environmental conditions in cities were improved dramatically. The process was often slow, but over time, many epidemic diseases have been controlled, the supply of clean water and the removal of wastes have become routine, the risks of fire have been contained and standards of comfort and cleanliness have risen to unprecedented levels. Cities could not have become as large and as numerous as they are now if environmental conditions had remained unchanged.

In a curious way, the pollution that cities suffer is largely due to their wealth. The rich consume a great deal more energy, water, building materials and other goods than the poor, and thus produce much more waste. This is what is happening, in the cities where rapid industrialisation is taking place—only the rich enjoy the benefits of piped water and refuse collection.

Increasingly Insanitary Conditions

There is another, often tragic, aspect to this situation.

The poorest of the poor are reduced to living in outer-edge shantytowns in extremely insanitary conditions and lacking the resources to deal with the problem, the city as a whole has to endure congestion and air and water pollution. Some towns and cities are expanding at a rate of over 7 per cent a year, municipal sanitation departments are no longer able to cope, and it is estimated that as many 30 per cent of the population are without running water.

In many of the world's major cities runaway population growth, an epidemic of Aids and rising social tensions have been combined in the last few years with a steep drop in incomes. The population living on the outer edges of the cities continues to grow apace, hundreds of thousands of people are without running water and 15 per cent of them without sanitation of any sort. Various voluntary bodies and non-governmental organisations have got together, often successfully.

Water and the Environmental Crisis

One key problem concerns the availability of clean water. Some progress has been achieved as a result of the International Drinking Water Supply and Sanitation Decade, but in 1994 at least 220 million people still lacked a source of drinking water near their homes. In some cases, communities of 500 or more inhabitants are served by a single tap. In some towns, communal taps function for only a few hours a day, so that people cannot build up sufficient reserves of water for their personal needs if it takes too long to fetch or if the water has to be carried long distances.

As there are no proper sanitation measures, the disadvantaged members of the population have to drink dirty water, fish in polluted stream and eat vegetables that have been grown by the side of refuse tips.

A further major problem arises from the three-fold harmful impact of cities on the environment: urban development on agricultural land, the extraction and exhaustion of natural resources and the dumping of refuse.

Growing pressure on coastal regions, where nearly a billion people now live, is doing serious damage to the marine environment. Development activities pose a threat to nearly half the world's coasts.

Towns originally offered people a place of refuge, of mutual help and culture. According to nineteenth century town-planning theorists, they should supply all human needs. They were supposed to be the very stuff of civilisation. That was not to be, and therefore whenever the authorities throw in their hands, dismayed by the scale of the problems and lacking the political will, money or resources to cope with them, personal initiatives are those most likely to succeed.

5

In Defence of the City Urban Development a Key for Survival

The figures sound alarming. The towns and cities in developing countries are growing faster than ever before. By the year 2000, 2.2 billion people will live in the cities of the Third World. Their numbers are expected to double by the year 2025. But many of the cities in Africa, Asia and Latin America are already bursting at the seams. Some of the so-called megacities have more than 10 or 15 million inhabitants. Many of them live in unplanned squatter settlements, without water and electricity, in an environment of squalor, poverty, crime and disease. Nevertheless, the cities seem to have lost nothing of their attraction for the rural populations. Although the larger share of the population increase in the cities of developing countries is caused by the children of people already living there, the rural-urban migration continues unabated. The cities still offer better chances for employment and education, they provide a better physical infrastructure, better health facilities and a more interesting life. Miserable as conditions in the cities often appear to be, they are usually much better than those in the rural areas. It is, therefore, an illusion to believe that the growth of the cities could be checked by concentrating the development efforts on the countryside. There is no alternative to urban development in a world will soon count some 8 billion people.

Cities have always been in the vanguard of development. The ancient civilisations of Mesopotamia, Egypt, Greece and

Rome were city cultures which for the first time in human development created large, well-governed states. In Europe during the Middle Ages, the creation of towns and cities offered the rural populations a chance to evade the oppression by feudal authorities and become free citizens. Local self-government in medieval towns is at the cradle of democratic development. There is a clear separation of competence between thc national, state and local level of government leaving citizens an opportunity to decide on matters which directly affect their own local environment. It is worth looking at this model when discussing ways organised to improve city governance and allow for more participation of the population.

Another fact worth looking at is the size of cities in industrialised countries. Although about three quarters of the people live in urban areas, there are only a handful of really big cities.

Of course, the growth of towns and cities in developed countries is the result of a long historical process, deeply rooted in the particular political and economic conditions of the past centuries. In developing countries today, other conditions prevail which favour the emergence of ever bigger urban conglomerations. However, governments are able, thorough appropriate investments and the location of industries educational facilities or housing policies to influence the settlement trends in their respective countries in favour of smaller cities.

One point seems certain, though, when considering the pros and cons of city development: the severe environmental problems facing mankind today can only be solved if people live in highly concentrated settlements rather than being spread out evenly over the whole countryside. Environment-friendly mass transport, for instance, is only possible in the cities. Fossil fuel consumption which adds to the pollution of the atmosphere will be lower when people live close to their places of work. Their supply with food, water, electricity and social amenities is cheaper and uses up fewer resources when distances are short. The use of land for housing, transport and industry is less when buildings grow in height rather than space. Even refuse disposal and wastewater management is easier to organise in a big city than in the countryside.

What is important then is not to question the validity of city development, but to make cities and tows a better place to live in. Good city governance, more involvement of the population in decision-making, more attention paid to environmental hazards caused by congestion and low safety standards are some of the demands that must be met to cope with the problems of the cities. There is no reason to bedevil the city as the most successful form of human settlement. Since the times of Babylon, it has also been a place where many different peoples and cultures meet. A generation from now, half the human population will live in cities. We should see this as a chance for human survival.

****

6

Innovative Milieus—Cities

Cities provide the local bases for international linkages. This is where the virtual worlds of highly specified communication networks are anchored. Complicating matters, globalisation and urbanisation have certain features in common. They challenge the existing order, constantly frustrate planning and emphasise plurality. Tension is the norm, cannot be avoided, and must, therefore, be handled constructively. Not coincidentally, however, cities posses civilising qualities: their very existence depends on reducing levels of violence.

Globalisation and urbanisation are two trends characterising the present. These two phenomena are closely linked because globalisation means that global networks emerge, which have their nodes in cities. The networks are heterogeneous, frequently based on competition and provide the stuff of which conflicts are made. At stake are cash flows, transnational companies, international civil society, migrant groups, religious communities, multilateral politics and cultural interdependencies. Nor should one forget the challenges of organised transnational crime or global terrorism. This is where global interests seek to maximize profits, but also where local grassroots and civil society develop new claims to assert rights to liveable urban space.

Global Cities

Global cities are defined as locations, which support international networking. They are under particular pressure and it sometimes even seems doubtful whether a global city can be treated as a single, coherent entity at all. There is a prevailing trend towards fragmentation because of the permanent competition of various norms and values, identities and social realities. This trend is exacerbated when populations organise in various local networks. On the other hand, the global networks use virtual habitats with far-reaching rules of largely homogeenous quality. In this sense, financial markets, for example, command their own virtual cities—as do heroin or cocaine dealing. Such virtual contexts, are, in turn, locally embedded in real cities. They dominate some neighbourhood but hardly affect others.

The traditional concept of "world cities" is passe. The notion referred to command centres with transnational significance and cosmopolitan culture. However, the hierarchy of various urban functions is no longer stable or permanent. Whereas the world city was viewed as control centre of the modern world system, the global city is integrated in distinctive global networks, none of which can automatically be assumed to be dominant, structuring or even yielding to the national government. Rather, we are dealing with distinct realities which are compatible only to various degrees and sometimes even incompatible. Global cities are characterised by confusion, because their various realities can no longer be integrated into a single system.

Global cities, moreover, contribute to our planet's environmental crisis. The size of airports is a good indicator of how global any particular agglomeration has become. On the other hand, air travel is a major, unregulated source of greenhouse emissions. Petrochemical fuels, on which most cities thrive, are the world market's core commodity.

In addition, large urban agglomerations are often located on the most fertile land and thus there extension reduces agricultural production. Every urban centre depends on food from outside, stimulating not only traffic but also intensive production in the hinterland, which in turn, has also become international. After all the pineapples on display in

Frankfurt's supermarkets do not grow in Germany, nor can the citizens of Toronto consume domestically produced lemons and oranges. It must be considered, however, how sustainability of natural resources would be challenged, if instead of population concentrations, we had highly overpopulated rural region in need of adequate infrastructure.

Cities have always served diverse cultures as arenas for encounter and exchange and accordingly, also as arenas of conflict. This applies to contemporary global cities more than ever before. Nevertheless, they are more than just articulation nodes of transnational networks. In view of the fact that the world is divided into territorial states, cities also belong to national political systems, for which they normally play distinct and decisive roles. Fashion, trends and other types of societal change have always originated from cities. Modern representative democracy was born of the cities-key historical events such as the Storming of the Bastille and the Boston Tea Party provide the evidence. On the other hand, state institutions are based in cities, from the national tax administration to judicial authority. A further aspect is social starification, because a nation's elite usually lives in the major cities.

Of course, not all of a city's people and communities are integrated in global networks. Social contexts with specific local histories, which different from the realisations of global networks, are equally relevant. In the cities local, national and global phenomena inter-relate. Executive managers with worldwide spheres of activity depend on their maids who-particularly, but not only, in poor countries—may hardly ever leave the household.

Traditionally, the urbanisation debate revolved around the experience of those nations that industrialised early. Empirical research normally looks at the aglomerations in Europe, North America and Japan, where the respective histories have national characteristics. In contrast, the development of Singapore, Kuala Lumpur or Jakarta resulted from colonialism. The dynamism of their growth was, from the outset, associated with global networks.

To this day, Third World Cities tend to be much more diverse than most OECD cities. While nationalism served as a central mechanism to integrate the urban populations in Europe in the 19th century, similar efforts in the colonial cities were regarded as a threat and suppressed as effectively as possible. Consequently, it is still common to find urban cultures in which rural places of origin define identities. People relate to their "homeland", which may be thousands of kilometres away and which some may not visit in their lifetime, rather than with the immediate neighbours they meet everyday.

All cities have their own history resulting in particular features. Urbanistion becomes specific in each city, but is likely to also affect other regions, because cities never exist in isolation. They always belong to systems of various corresponding centres, because population groups pursue the same interests, or, at least, related interests. This typically is expressed in architecture, with the result that, even today, one can still find traces of the Northern Italian Renaissance in small towns of other countries.

Moreover, urbanisation implies a civilising process. To exist in the long term, cities must curb violence, despite the diverse nature of their populations and their conflicting interests. Wherever that is not done successfully, cities become irrelevant fast. The connection between civilising and urbanism is based on two pillars. These are firstly the public sphere and political deliberation and, secondly, something I have described elsewhere as "locality". Locality ensures social control through personal contacts and interlinking institutions. It is not about communities or districts, but networks of relationships which are integrated through various activities. Locality arises from initiative and self organisation and can hardly be orchestrated by administrations. Locality and public sphere complement each other. Otherwise, selfcreated and self-regulated interactions could not persist under the pressure of real estate speculation, official town planning, and other dominant societal forces.

The World Bank holds a similar view. Its Urban Peace Programme zeroes in on strategies to reduce violence. The focus is on supporting local communities in an effort to increase "social capital". In a similar vein, violence erodes social capital, as it reduces trust and cooperation within formal and informal social organisations that are critical for a society to function.

Planning Paralysis

The rapid growth of many cities makes building social capital particularly important. There must be scope for creative and cooperative improvisation, because local authorities are often strikingly overburdened. The enormous size of mega-cities with several million inhabitants makes it clear that comprehensive control and even planning are impossible. In many cases, civil servants do not even notice that new slums have formed within a few years, which may easily have more inhabitants than large towns. Such developments make the demand for better planning obsolete from the outset. Too often, we do not really know what makes mega-cities tick.

It is clear that private enterprise steps in where profits are attractive. This applies to local business but also to multinational corporations. Well-known examples are provided in the construction industry, building homes, offices, factories and roads. But schools and hospitals are also operated privately. Without private bus, and in some places, even rail companies, traffic would collapse completely. Lucrative mobile telephone markets are expanding, where the conventional fixed line telephone network has been overburdened for decades. Electricity and water supply offer opportunities, both for multinational companies smelling profit and for slum dwellers attempting to tap utility services for free.

It is not uncommon for clashes to occur with city authorities. What official regulations demand often makes little sense to the firm engaged or the people affected.

Influential persons are often involved in the private companies, which helps to avoid official rules or to have them rewritten. Whether corruption takes place or formal decision processes are adhered to, may make surprisingly little difference on the ground. Typically very little attention is paid to the needs of poor people.

Nevertheless, urban life offers opportunities for economic, political and cultural participation even for marginalised people. This is what leads to rural-urban migration in the first place. Admittedly, it also means tough competition for housing space. There is ever-increasing demand for shelter. At the same time, the public and private sector are neither interested in, nor in a position to fulfill the right to an adequate shelter. The poor urban population can improve its fate only in the slums and often only using its own initiative—such as through locally supported microfinance schemes to get legal access to land.

This kind of societal creativity in initiative and self-organisation is not limited to the production of housing. It is also visible in petty trading and the informal sector, which blossom in economic niches and continues to discover new niches. Among the fields of activity are waste recycling, domestic services or, of course, drug peddling, "Innovative milieus" are not only found in business high-rises, universities and research institutes. They are also prolific in slums markets and even on garbage dumps.

Initiative, self-organisation and social creativity have political consequences. Communal self-determination and the building up of local organisations depend on democratic principles. Formal participation is relevant—but so is scope for informal improvisation. The relevance of grassroots activity is one reason for totalitarian and authoritarian regimes always looking at cities with great scepticism. Revolts and protest movements normally start in the urban centres. How political challenges are dealt with, on the other hand, sets precedents, which define what is normal and to be expected. This is institution building in practical terms. It happens spontaneously and unplanned with long-term consequences far beyond the city limits. Periods of rapid growth, moreover, are particularly critical because they are, by definition, times of rapid change.

Conclusion

Things often happen in unplanned and disorderly ways in cities and agglomerations. Especially in poor countries, the living conditions are often anything but idylic. Nevertheless, there is no alternative in the development process but to build on this difficult foundation. Inspite of all the dirt, misery and hardship, urban environments offer prospects not only of survival but also of participation, democratic modernisation and civilisation (in the basic sense of reducing violent interaction). That people are flocking into the cities proves that these places attractive in spite of their dismal slums, overflowing drains and congested traffic. It is telling that it is so rare, in poor countries, to see anyone return to their rural homes for good.

Globalisation accelerates the dynamics described above, while urbanisation is, at the same time providing the base for making international networks ever more important. Both trends are interrelated. They imply that city life is gaining relevance in economic, political and cultural terms with the influence of specific urban settings potentially spreading far beyond the borders of the nation-state, without, however, making urbanisation more predictable or even more amendable to planning. On the contrary: the potential for conflict is growing.

* * * *

7

Population Growth and Urbanisation

The world's cities are growing far faster than its population. Indeed, aside from the growth of population itself, urbanisation is the dominant demographic trend of the half-century now ending. In 1950, 750 million of the world's people lived in cities. By 1996, this had at least tripled, to more than 2.6 billion. The number projected to live in cities by 2050, some 6.5 billion people, exceeds world population today.

Urbanisation on anything like the scale that we know today is historically quite recent. In 1800, only one city, London, had a million people. Today, 326 cities have at least that many people. And there are 14 mega cities, those with 10 million or more residents. Tokyo is the largest, at 27 million. Mexico city is second, at 17 million. New York city and Sao Paulo are close behind, with 16 million each. Rounding out the list in descending size are Mumbai (15 million), Shanghai (14), Los Angeles (12), Kolkata (12), Buenos Aires (12), Beijing (11), Osaka (11), Lagos (10), Rio de Janeiro (10), and Delhi (10).

The rate of growth of cities in industrial countries during the first century or so of the Industrial Revolution was relatively slow. Today's cities are growing much faster. It took London 130 years to get from 1 million to 8 million. Mexico city made this jump in just 30 years.

Measured in annual growth, some cities, such as Lagos, Nigeria, are growing at 5 per cent a year; Mumbai is growing at nearly 4 per cent. The world's urban population as a whole is growing by just over 1 million people each week. This urban growth is fed by natural increase of urban populations, by net migration from the countryside, and by villages, by net migration from the countryside, and by villages or towns expanding to the point where they become cities or they are absorbed by the spread of existing cities.

During the early stages of industrialisation, urbanisation was largely in response to the pull of employment opportunities in cities. More recently, however, the movement from countryside to city has been more the result of rural push than of urban pull. It is a reflection of the lack of opportunity in the countryside as already small plots of land are divided and then divided again with each passing generation, until they become so small that people can no longer make a living from them.

Historically, cities and the surrounding countryside had a symbolic relationship, with the latter supplying food and raw materials in exchange for manufactured products. Today, cities are tied much more to each other and to the global economy. The food and fuel that once came from the surrounding countryside now often comes from distant corners of the planet.

As societies urbanize, the use of basic resources, such an energy and water rises. In traditional rural societies, for example, people live on the land and thus do not need to travel to work. But once they migrate to cities, commuting becomes the rule, not the exception. In villages, most of the food that is consumed is produced locally, requiring little energy for processing, packaging, and transportation; once people move into cities, on the other hand, virtually all their food must be brought in. In a village where residents typically draw their water from a central well and carry it to their homes, water use in necessarily limited. But when villagers move to urban high-rise apartment buildings with indoor plumbing, replete with showers and flush toilets, water consumption soars.

The ecology of cities is a continuing challenge to city managers simply because cities require the concentration of huge quantities of water, food, energy and raw materials. The waste products must then be dispersed or the city will become uninhabitable. As cities become larger, the disposal of residential and industrial wastes becomes ever more challenging.

Partly as a result of the mounting pressure for people to migrate to cities, the growth in urban populations is far out stripping the availability of basic services, such as water, sewerage, transportation, and electricity. As a result, life in urban shantytowns is plagued by poverty, pollution, congestion, homelessness, and unemployment.

Since the beginning of the Industrial Revolution, the terms of trade between countryside and city have favoured the latter simply because cities control the scarce resources in development, namely capital and technology. But if the price of food rises in the years ahead, as now seems likely, the terms of trade could shift, favouring the countryside. If in the new world of the twenty-first century the scarce resources are land and water, those controlling them could have the upper hand in determining rural/urban terms of trade.

This aside, if recent trends continue, within the next several years more than half of us will be living in cities—making the world more urban than rural for the first time in history. We will have become an urban species, far removed from our hunter-gatherer origins.

****

8

Land Tenure

Securing Land for the Urban Poor

Around the world, especially in Asia and Africa, towns and cities are expanding rapidly. For the poorest people, finding affordable, safe and secure urban land for shelter has become increasingly difficult. This is because:

- Overall competition for land makes it increasingly costly;
- Central urban areas are being developed for commercial use;
- Natural features such as mountains or swamps limit physical urban expansion; and
- Meeting land management and planning standards (concerned with legality, technical and administrative accuracy) is expensive.

As a result, a large and increasing proportion of urban populations are forced to live in peripheral areas or occupy marginalised and dangerous locations. These settlements are often illegal and, providing inadequate shelter and lacking essential services only exacerbate the problems of the poor. Higher levels of ill health, unemployment and non-sustainable land-use often result. Furthermore, residents may also be under constant threat of eviction by government and exploitation by landowners.

Experience shows that, if residents in such areas feel secure and safe from eviction, they do over time improve their neighbourhoods. Recognition of, and granting of secure forms of tenure to previously illegal settlements often provides the incentive to communities to invest their resources in upgrading their housing and wider neighbourhoods. Security of tenure also brings the improved likelihood of basic infrastructure and other essential community services.

There is a wide range of urban land tenure systems. In many urban areas, including areas designated illegal by government, there are informal or customary tenure systems—these are often the commonest form of tenure and are expanding most rapidly.

While statutory or "legal" forms of tenure (for example freehold or leasehold agreements) offer many advantages, such as full individual rights and security and access to formal credit systems, they can also cause the very problems they were intended to solve:

- Higher rental levels, which may displace existing renters;
- The selling out of the secure land to higher income groups;
- Encouragement of new illegal/informal settlements, as the poorest hope that they will also eventually get security of tenure;
- Encouragement of landowners and developers to hold land, without investing in its improvement or paying taxes on its increased value—which serves to attract even greater levels of investment and land price inflation.

In addition, if peoples' income remain low and the capacity of the banks or credit unions is weak, statutory forms of tenure alone may not necessarily stimulate neighbourhood improvements.

Consequently, careful analysis of existing systems of informal and customary tenure and property right is required, before embarking on major land management and tenure reforms. These can provide both acceptable levels of security and access to credit, which in turn stimulate improvements to local neighbourhoods. Before any decisions are made, tenure policies must recognise the likely impact on tenants, the poor and other vulnerable groups, especially women.

For these reasons, it is sometimes better to increase the rights of residents (e.g., by protecting them from the threat of forced evictions, or by increasing their access to essential utilities or credit), rather than assuming that they need freehold or leasehold titles.

Strategies for providing shelter now recognise the diverse nature of needs, and the positive contribution which decent housing makes to social and economic development at both national and local levels. They also recognise that the most effective way of mobilising the resources required is to encourage investment in housing by individuals, communities and the private sector.

Recent experience shows that many governments are now introducing positive approaches, which are market-sensitive and encourage more efficient use of available land. These include measures to encourage landowners and developers to allocate a specified proportion of units to low-income groups out of profits generated from planning permission granted by (and therefore partly created by) the government. Public-private partnerships and revisions to planning standards and administrative procedures have also demonstrated that it is possible to reduce the costs of access to land for the poor even under conditions of market-led development, thus reducing urban sprawl, the occurrence of slum settlements and levels of poverty.

****

9

Living with Leviathan

In the year 2015, there will mega-cities with more than 8 million inhabitants—22 of them in Asia. How will they cope? Humanity is about to set a new record. Nearly two-thirds of the planet's population will be living in cities by 2025, UN population experts say. Until now, rural people have outnumbered city-dwellers.

World population, according to the same projections, will top eight billion in 25 year's time, including five billion in cities. The increase will be particularly spectacular in the cities of the developing world, whose total population will double to four billion. We are going to see an unprecedented exodus of people from rural areas.

The demographer's predictions are only tentative of course. But the flow of people into megacities in developing countries is well under way. Several sociological changes are behind it.

Cities used to need muscle-power for the jobs they provided, the experts point out. But today they no longer attract people just because of their economic potential. There is plenty of evidence that they can go on steadily attracting people even when the job-generating sectors are in bad shape or disappearing.

People no longer move to urban centres because they are fairly sure to find work. They do so because they want to leave the countryside where there are too many people tilling the land and because they hope to leave poverty behind. Rightly or wrongly, the city seems to offer progress and freedom, a vision of opportunity, an irresistible lure.

The result is that both inside and outside cities, there are more and more squatters and poor housing. Urbanisation in the developing world differs from that in the industrialised countries, in "the speed of the process, the growth of poverty, the extent of urban sprawl and the expansion of the informal economy."

How are the authorities in the developing world's urban areas responding to such "invasions"? In today's deregulated world, the trend is to question the very idea of providing the general population with basic urban services, most observers note. For want of resources, cities in developing countries are increasingly abandoning their public service function.

China is still an exception to this in several ways. Officials there, in a context of rigid planning—though this has eased in recent years—are trying to prevent the influx of more rural migrants than the city economies can cope with, as the example of Shanghai shows. Can such a policy, which works fairly well for the moment, survive the political and economic hangs under way?

At the other end of the scale is Lagos (Nigeria), whose expansion is chaotic, about 200 slums have sprung up in this African city. Every now and then, one of them is bulldozed without notice and without heed for its inhabitants. But Lagos survives, thanks to the vibrant ingenuity of its millions of citizens. Another revealing city is Jakarta, where the authorities themselves have joined in frantic property speculation. As a result of this speculation, more than 4.5 million people have been evicted from their homes in the last 30 years, with little compensation, to make possible the construction of high-rise blocks, which sometimes stand empty.

How do the original inhabitants of a city react to the massive influx of people from outside? In more and more cities, you see smart neighbourhood protected by guard—called "fortress-cities". In these fortified enclaves, built partly in response to real or imagined lack of security, the roads, sewage system, schools and other community services are private. Outside them, public areas have been abandoned to the least fortunate members of the society and the infrastructure there is crumbling or inadequate. The middle and poorer classes also defend themselves in their own neighbourhoods. One surprising case can be found in the satellite cities just outside Brasilia, where iron railing protect the houses, from fancy villas to the humblest shack.

Will the mega-cities of the 21st century be made up of islands of "social tribes"—"anticities" of walled enclaves, whose wealthy residents refuse to pay taxes to provide facilities for the city's less fortunate inhabitants? Will cities still integrate their inhabitants?

"The existence of a slum means the authorities have failed," says the World Bank. The bank encourages projects where the state and the private sector join hands to help the less fortunate buy plots of land in areas with an infrastructure. Other experts say the "anti-social" aspects of globalisation should be blamed. They would like to see the big cities of the next century return to their original function as a crossroads and a meeting-place.

****

10

Climate Change and Human Health

Changes in the India's climate, stemming from the greenhouse effect, are highly likely to damage human health. Food and fresh water supplies will be disrupted, millions of people displaced, and disease patterns altered dangerously and unpredictably.

Human health could be affected by even quite small changes in average mean temperature, and there is the prospect of some major diseases flourishing in warmer conditions and of more resistant strains of infection emerging.

The population in India most vulnerable to the negative impacts of global warming are in the lower-income groups, residents of coastal lowlands and islands, those living in semi-arid lands, and the urban poor in the squatter settlements, slums and shanty towns of large cities.

Present strategies for immunisation, coping with disease vectors or carriers, providing safe drinking water, and improving nutrition are all based on existing climate regimes, ecosystems, and sea and solar radiation levels. These are all expected to change, but exactly how much cannot be predicted. It is therefore, virtually impossible to adjust health and nutritional strategies to take account of possible climate changes.

Humans can adapt to moderate changes in temperature and to occasional extremes. But this adaptive capacity is relatively low in infants and the elderly; it rises through childhood and adolescence to reach a maximum which can be maintained up to about 30 years of age.

A changing climate would alter the ecosystems of the vectors or agents which carry or cause many diseases, whether these be viruses, bacteria, parasites, plants, insects or other animals such as mosquitoes and snails. As the weather warms, the boundaries of the tropics may extend into the present subtropics, and parts of temperate areas may become subtropical. As air temperature increase, some diseases will become common in regions which once rarely knew them and where there is little natural resistance to them. As a result, death rates may also climb significantly.

It is possible that warmer weather around the world will cause increases in summer diseases and decreases in those associated with winter. Diseases contracted from both water and air will also spread more readily as ambient temperature rise. In a warmer climate, mosquitoes and other vectors also may migrate vertically up into highlands which were once too cold for them. This may be particularly hazardous in tropical highland areas where there is no natural resistance to malaria.

Changes in temperature, rainfall, humidity and storm patterns may affect diseases borne by vectors in two ways. First, they will directly affect the vector's reproduction rate, biting rate, and the duration and frequency of human exposure. Second, they may modify agricultural systems or plant species, thus changing the relationship between host and vector. Development rates of malarial mosquitoes, for example, increase with warmer temperatures, but these pests need wet areas in which to breed.

Sea-level rise could also spread infectious diseases by flooding sewerage and sanitation systems in coastal cities, and increase the incidence of diarrhoea in children. The flooding of hazardous waste dumps and sanitation systems could lead to long-term contamination of croplands.

Rising seas may also disrupt marine habitats land aquatic food chains. Since fish constitute 40 per cent of all animal protein consumed by the people of India such a disruption of the marine ecosystem would affect the food supplies of many millions of people and dramatically increase protein deficiency and malnutrition. Changes in the availability of food and water, as well as radical shifts in disease patterns, could initiate large migrations of people, exacerbating food shortages, overcrowding, social stress and instability.

Some of the factors contributing significantly to global warming, such as the burning of fossil fuels and the use of chlorofluorocarbons (CFCs) and halons, threaten human health in other ways too. A typical petrol-driven motor car, for example, emits carbon monoxide, sulphur and nitrogen oxides, hydrocarbons, low-level ozone and lead—all of which are hazardous to health.

The ozone-depleting CFCs and halons pose a particular threat to humans through an increased risk of skin cancer, cataracts and lower immunity to other illnesses as a result of increased exposure to ultraviolet B radiation from the sun. Skin cancer risks are expected to rise most among fair-skinned.

11

Climate Politics After Kyoto

Solidarity Understood Correctly

The Kyoto Protocol does not do enough to protect humankind from climate change. Additional binding reduction targets for greenhouse gases are necessary and they must also apply to important developing and transition countries. So far, these countries have been treated as a uniform group. In future, different rules will have to be used according to varying capabilities and different exposures to risk.

The Kyoto Protocol climate protection came into force internationally in February. At its core are binding commitments for industrialised countries to restrict their greenhouse gas emissions. This is an important step—however, it is only the first one in coming to terms with the challenge of the century: climate protection. The reduction targets of five per cent on average for advanced nations established so far are insufficient. Moreover, there are no obligations yet for developing and transition countries, which emit almost half of the greenhouse gases worldwide.

At the climate summit in Buenos Aires the European Union tried to kick-start negotiations on the further development of the Kyoto Protocol with moderate success. While the negotiations in the run-up to Kyoto were already quite difficult, the new phase of international climate politics that is just beginning presents even greater obstacles. Apart from reintegrating the climate—desperado USA into the international process, future negotiations will have to involve several transition and developing countries.

However, these countries point to the rich nations' historic responsibility for ongoing climate change. They are afraid their economic development might be slowed down. Meanwhile, many of the poorer developing countries are particularly vulnerable. Due to their geographical location, economic structure and weak financial and technical capacities, they are virtually, helplessly exposed to the consequences of the greenhouse effect. Therefore, future negotiations must break the "North-South" grid as well as find an adequate differentiation for the very heterogeneous countries of the "South"

The central theme of our work was the principle of solidaity. This implies that weak countries should be supported when tackling the effects of climate change. As started in Article 2 of the Framework convention of Climate Change, humankind's "dangerous" interference with the cli mate must be stopped. This means that global warming must be restricted to, at most, two centigrades above pre-industrial temperatures. Any warming above this level would threaten human existence in many regions. The cultural survival of local communities and the physical integrity of the weak and powerless would be acutely endangered.

Mitigation Becomes a Negotiation Topic

Even in keeping to this two degree mark, which the European union has adopted, impact of climate change, which is already noticeable now, would be aggravated further. The first conclusion of our team therefore is that future negotiations can no longer deal merely with combating the causes of the problem by redusing emissions. Talks have to go further and contribute to limiting damage. Measures to adapt to climate change, particularly in the case of very vulnerable countries, must play a central role.

In terms of finance, technology and personnel, many developing countries are in no position to adequately handle the negative consequences of climate change. They need transfer payments. Financing mechanisms that correspond to the "polluter pays" principle are inevitable—and introducing them is a precondition to move a head with preventive measures. Developing countries will only be prepared to accept reduction targets for emissions if the industrialised countries contribute (financially) to adapting to climate change. All summed up, however, reduction and prevention of greenhouse gases also serve adaptation programmes. The more effectively climate protection is implemented, after all, the lower the costs for adapting to the climate change will be—not to mention irreversible effects of climate change, such as the extinction of animal and plant species and the melting of glaciers.

If climate change is to be limited to two degrees Celsius on average globally humankind's emissions must peak by 2020, drop to half level reached in the 1990s by the middle of this century and then continue to decrease. There is widespread agreement among politicians, scientists civil society actors on the necessity of emission reductions. The difficulties begin with question of which countries are to contribute. When does their obligation begin and what extent does it have?

The Kyoto Protocol retains the categories outlined in the Framework Convention on Climate Change. Accordingly, the advanced Western nations and the former Soviet block form one group (Annex countries) and the rest of the World the second group (non-annex I countries). This is not practical in the long-term.

The Kyoto Protocol defines negotiated reduction obligations among the parties of the first group. Given the increasing contribution of the "rest of the world" to global emission levels, future regulations must also engage several transition and developing countries. To do so, it is necessary to differentiate more strongly between these countries—according to their capabilities and circumstances.

Criteria for Differential Treatment

In order to reflect the country—specific conditions in a fair manner, our proposal consider three criteria:

- the potential to reduce greenhouse gases;
- the capacity to finance reduction measures; and
- the responsibility for climate change.

In view of these criteria, the non-Annex I countries obviously differ greatly. As a matter of course, all countries with the lowest emissions per capita are included. However, so are several countries with the highest emissions per capita world wide—Qatar, for example. All least developed countries (LDC) fall into the category, but so do countries such as Singapore, with a per capita income well above the average of the industrialised countries. Obviously, it does not make sense to treat these countries as equals in climate talks.

If the "non Annex countries" are differentiated according to the three criteria mentioned above, four groups can be identified:

- Newly industrialising countries (NIC)
- Rapidly industrialising developing countries" (RIDC)
- Other developing countries (ODC)
- Least developed countries(LDC)

COUNTRY GROUPS

Newly Industrialised Countries—NICs

Bahrain, Brunei, Cuba, Kazakhastan, South Korea, Kuwait, Qatar, Saudi Arabia, Singapore, Suriname, Trinidad and Tobago, Turkmenistan, United Arab Emirates, Uzbekistan.

Rapidly Industrialising Developing Countries—RIDs

Algeria, Antigua & Barbuda, Argentina, Bahamas, Barbodos, Belize, Bosnia and Herzegovina, Botswana, Brazil,

Chile, China, Colombia, Costa Rica, Cyprus, Dominican Republic, El Salvador, Fiji, Grenada, Guyana, Iran, Jordan, Malaysia, Malta, Mauritius, Mexico, Oman, Panama, Peru, Philippines, Saint Kitts and Nevis, Saint Lucia, Saint Vincent and Grenadines, South Africa, Thailand, Tunisia, Uruguay.

Other Developing Countries—ODCs

Armenia, Azerbaijan, Bolivia, Cameroon, Congo, Cook Islands, Cote d'lovire, Dominica, Ecuador, Egypt, Gabon, Georgia, Ghana, Honduras, India, Indonesia, Jamaica, Kenya, Kyrgyzstan, Libya, Macedonia, FYR, Moldova, Mongolia, Morocco, Namibia, Nicaragua, Nige ria, Pakistan, Papua New Guinea, Paraguay, Seychelles, Sri Lanka, Swaziland, Syria, Tajikistan, Venezuela, Vietnam, Zimbabwe.

Least Developed Countries—LDCs

Afghanistan, Angola, Bangladesh, Benin, Bhutan, Burkina Faso, Burundi, Cambodia, Cape Verde, Central African Republic, Chad, Comoros, Democratic Republic of Congo, Djibouti, Equatorial Guinea, Eritrea, Ethiopia, Gambia, Guinea, Guinea-Bissau, Haiti, Kiribati, Laos, Lesotho, Liberia, Madagascar, Malawi, Maldives, Mali, Mauritania, Mozambique, Myanmar, Nepal, Niger, Rwanda, Samoa, Sao Tome and Principe, Senegal, Sierra Leone, Solomon Islands, Somalia, Sudan Tanzania, Togo, Tuvalu, Uganda, Vanuatu, Yemen, Zambia.

We are not interested in splitting the negotiating group of the "G 77 and China" politically. But solidarity among these countries requires that those which are better off make a contribution to global climate protection on a different scale than, for example, the LDCs. Only in this way can the group retain its important unity in negotiations with the advanced countries and, at the same time, tackle the climate problem.

What would the climate protection obligations of the different country groups look like in concrete terms? We propose the following rules:

- The potential to reduce emissions should determine binding reduction targets. This potential arises from the emission intensity of a country (CO_2 emitted per unit of the gross domestic product) and from the emissions per capita. This line of action would guarantee a cost efficient climate regime, since emissions would be reduced wherever the potential for doing so was highest. This does not necessarily mean, however, that the countries, concerned would be liable to fund all necessary measures. Certainly the industrial countries would have to contribute too.
- Obligations to finance climate protection would have to derive from the respective capacity of a country. This capacity could be measured against the average income and the Human Development Index. Countries with a higher capacity—mainly industrialised countries—would have to support those with lower capacity.
- To what extent obligations become binding should ultimately depend on a country's contribution to climate change. The accumulated emissions since 1990 could serve as a suitable indicator. At that time, the United Nations had already identified the greenhouse effect as a human-made problem.

These rules would mean that the advanced industrialised countries, and to a somewhat lesser degree also the former planned economies, would have to take on absolute, binding reduction targets going far beyond Kyoto.

Moreover, these Annex-I Countries would be bound to make transfer payments to the four other groups in support of climate protection. According to our proposal, the "newly industrialised countries" (NICs) and the "rapidly industrialising developing countries" (RIDCs) will also have to make an active, quantifiable contribution to reducing global emissions in the near future. The NICs could rely on rich nations co-financing some of their measures—and the RIDCs on broad funding of their climate protection by the advanced nations. Without such transfer payments, emission targets for NICs/RIDCs would not become binding. On the other hand, the remaining two groups (ODCs, LDCs) would have to gradually adopt policies and measures for a more climate-friendly direction of their development. Their burden will be to put their full efforts into adapting to climate change.

The key to the indispensable integration of the developing countries into a system of binding emission targets lies in differentiation. For this purpose, the existing country categories will have to be broken up. Even if many of the politicians of the G77 & China negotiating group still resist the idea, there were already clear indications in Buenos Aires that the unity of the group cannot be maintained without acknowledgement of its members' heterogeneity. The countries most affected by climate change will, for example, no longer tolerate the OPEC countries blocking payments for adaptation measures with compensation demands for possibly declining oil exports.

Several other G77 countries also gradually recognise the need to move on from the Kyoto Protocol. They are signaling willingness to negotiate. In the medium term, therefore, this group must seek unity in its multiplicity for its own sake and show concern for its own and show concern for the interests of its weaker members. Otherwise the group will lose the negotiating power required to gain necessary concessions from the advanced countries. It goes without saying that the latter have to lead the way in climate protection.

****

12

Heating up Environmental Education and Communication

Worldwide environmental issues ranging from the hazardous waste in your backyard to ozone depletion far away in the atmosphere can threaten our planet and compromise our quality of life. The positive and negative effects of environmental interactions are just beginning to be better understood and addressed. Within this context, environmental education and communication have a remarkable opportunity to accelerate understanding and to mobilise national and community participation in change.

Communication because it is the exchange of information. In social programmes, its effectiveness depends on assessing audience needs and taking into account the social, cultural and economic aspects of a problem as well as the quality of education messages and materials.

Education because it involves learning—learning how to think about an issue and its solution; how to acquire and refine skills for solving problems; how to transfer what is learned from situation to situation.

In social programmes, communication and education together lead to increased public participation in problem-solving and in activities which promote change. The participation of many individuals over time can lead to changed expectations for individual behaviour and institutional practices.

The process of communication and education together might be thought of as the "heating up" of a society around an issue through the "saturation" of all available channels of communication. In a "hot" society, all channels of communication and the processes of individual and social change reinforce a message. From the perspective of designing an education and communication programme, this might be called the "saturation" approach to social change.

Example of 'Saturation'

A decade ago, research information about the link between smoking and chronic disease, particularly cancer and heart attack, was communicated to health professionals in a hostile environment where smoking was considered socially "in". But information campaigns by governments and cancer/heart associations put smoking on the public agenda. The result? Conversations about smoking increased within households, doctors' offices and in laboratories. Community organisations began to take action. Schools and the work place joined in.

No-smoking campaigns became a catalyst for change in attitudes and behaviour in health with "smoking" as a unifying symbol. Under the umbrella of "smoking", the rituals and behaviours associated with smoking were individually affected by the saturation process. Therefore other health activities related to smoking also reaped the benefits. Extending the impact of saturation can be applied to other contexts.

Today, a new global image is emerging—an image which represents the environment and unifies people behind its common cause. The symbol of a "Green" earth and the colour "green" are perpetuating an environmental movement, the result of and an inspiration to environmental education and communication efforts everywhere.

"Green" political parties are gaining popular support. All over the world "green" label marketing approaches are influencing consumer behaviour. Just as in the smoking example, acting upon the unifying symbol of "green" through environmental education and communication has the potential to strengthen programmes and further heat up public consciousness. Environmental education and communication provides the opportunity to support policy change, institutional change and behaviour change in highly segmented audiences.

Stage 1: Setting the Public Agenda

Globally, the public is already talking about the environment. Numerous single-issue environmental groups and educational programmes are already in operation. People become ready to talk about, think about and support environmental activities. Membership in existing environmental groups increases, and new programmes and opportunities for popular participation appear.

Stage 2: Engaging Key Institutions

Building alliances and collaboration among institutions creates a network. Lead institutions reach out to other institutions representing social process—education, work, religion and government—and initiate collaborative educational activities. For example, school systems integrate environmental modules within existing curricula and initiate teacher training and youth ecoclubs. Community based action increasingly addresses local issues such as garbage collection and industrial pollutants. Media coverage responds more frequently and positively.

Stage 3: Establishing a New Environmental Order

Governmental and non-governmental institutions become the initiators of environmental education, and participation becomes broader and more diverse. Specific target audiences begin to modify their role with regard to particular environmental problems. Community mobilisation increasingly generates demand for appropriate regulatory change. Expectations for appropriate individual and social behaviour begin to change. Finally, "Green" positions become "in", "non-Green" positions "out".

Applied Research

Experience with development communication in other sectors leads to optimism in reaching new levels of excellence in combining environmental education and communication. Perhaps the most important element in "putting it all together", however, is to maintain commitment to well-tried applied research procedures.

- Investigation of target audience characteristics (including socio-economic, gender and cultural) and attributes (attitudinal and behavioural) in relation to local environmental issues provides insight into an appropriate model of behaviour change and effective educational strategies, messages and materials.
- Limited testing of innovative strategies devised for local situations will uncover refinements needed for broader application.
- Comparison studies between the impact of different educational strategies with similar objectives will provide a basis for future strategic choices.
- Standardised indicators of impact and evaluation studies will provide an assessment of the progress and impact of programmes and, to some extent, the relative power of different components within the programmes.
- Content analyses of mass media over time will provide profiles of societies "heating up" on environmental issues.
- Description of the differences between industrialised country and developing country objectives, programme content and impact will provide a source of new insight about the process of social and individual change.

In addition, applied research can also advance the state of the art for environmental education and communication when properly field tested. There are two major sources for such innovation:

1. the refinement of social change theory at universities and research firms;
2. "creative" concepts with proved efficacy in other sectors such as the "enter-educate" approach (education through entertainment) in the population sector.

This description of the potential and progress of environmental education and communication is, in reality, a call to action. The "heating up" of societies on environmental issues is technically within our reach through environmental education and communication programmes. It is up to us to develop the funding, the research-based strategies—and the communication among professionals about results, both successes and failure—required to make it happen.

13

Health Care Relief in Conflict Situations
What Can We Learn from the Food Relief Experience?

Conflicts and war occur in many of the poorest nations where populations already suffer from severe ill-health. War leads to an increase in disease and to a worsening of the already fragile condition of populations. Health care itself becomes a victim of conflict. Many deaths which occur during these emergencies are not discretely related to the conflict itself but are the result of lacking access to public health services. Furthermore, conflict itself but are the result of lacking access to public health services. Furthermore, conflict contributes to the deterioration of already pre-existing structural weaknesses of the health care system. An example is the period of internal conflict in Uganda (1970-86) when health services declined in the aftermath of the war due to the impact of foreign assistance and the planning vacuum in which the activities took place.

The Impact of Conflict on Health Care

Conflict and civil strife may lead to a major disruption of health services. This is not only a result of physical destruction but also of finding shortages since national governments increase spending on military activities. Casualties increase the demand for curative services which can divert already limited resources from preventive care.

In the case of the Sudanese civil war a large majority of health professionals were forced to abandon rural health services and left for urban areas or neighbouring countries in order to find new employment. Entire preventive health services such as immunisation as well as water and sanitation projects collapsed leaving the population exposed to infectious diseases and epidemics. In urban areas, the gap in public health care provision is sometimes filled with the expansion of private services. In rural areas, private sector involvement in health care is rather marginal, apart from some omission hospitals or pharmacies. Therefore the non-formal health care sector often makes a substantial contribution towards health care.

With the rise of internal conflicts in Africa, more people suffer from emergency situations. This also increases the influence and impact of international donors. External assistance now a days accounts for more than 25 per cent of government health expenditure in Sub-Saharan Africa.

The size of donor involvement reflects the power of international agencies to control the policy domain. Countries in conflict or post-conflict situations are under pressure to 'rescue' their health systems and accept global policies in exchange for aid assistance and relief.

However, in the period after 1991, donor organisations tended to increase their expenditures for high profile humanitarian operations rather than ordinary development activities. This shift may reflect the increasing influence of media covering some of the conflicts. Too often, organisations intervene with ad hoc assistance without sufficient consultation at local level.

Donors' Perceptions in Designing Relief Interventions

Today, in many parts of Sub-Saharan Africa development assistance has virtually collapsed and has been substituted by relief assistance. The problem is that relief interventions are based on a western construction of reality, reflecting what is desirable and necessary in times of conflict.

Most interventions therefore stress physical and material needs, presuming that the social aspect of food and health is not an immediate issue to address.

The question which arises here is on who's views and perceptions these needs are based? While donors interest may be guided from the perspective of ill-health, the recipient government may be concerned with the collapse of the economy. However, any intervention needs to take into account that local knowledge and practices are shaped by state interests as well as power relationships. The common belief that health care systems always collapse due to conflict is sometimes mistaken. Considering the fact that today's internal conflicts are often fragmented, conflicts do not necessarily result in a breakdown of the health care delivery system.

Donors tend to respond with a 'package' approach and developing countries ministries of health increasingly play a symbolic role. The evidence suggests that international organisations tend to create vertical programmes which undermine national public health programmes. Foreign interventions are technically sophisticated and reorienting health are towards a more curative approach. Too little attention given to strengthen the health care system within its own limits, providing more appropriate technology, drugs and emphasizing the training of local health staff.

Another vital issue concerns the existence of already fragile health information systems. Agencies tend to bring their own systems which leads to further fragmentation. The local perspective on what are the 'basic needs' in physical and social health are usually not considered. Health relief interventions do not recognize the potential of the communities and the non-formal health sector such as healers and traditional midwifes in supporting and maintaining health care sector presents a substantial contribution towards health. It is not the question between choosing either allopathic or traditional services, it is more the decision which kind of illness will be best treated by which practitioner.

There is a need in further exploring the role of this sector particularly since this is sometimes the only service available for certain populations.

Responding to Local Needs

More community-based public health interventions could be vital to reduce mortality and morbidity. For example, in Somalia during the 1992 war and famine high mortality rates due to measles and diarrhoea could has been prevented by involving the communities in primary health care activities such as immunisation and nutrition improvement.

In the African context Tigray is an example where health services had been sustained and partially expanded during the civil war against the Ethiopian government. Local government structures called Baitos promoting social and economic development. Baitos encouraged communities to establish revolving funds for drugs and medical equipment. It actually functioned as an early type of community financing system.

As mentioned above, the challenge in changing health care relief strategies is to overcome the approach of short-term interventions, particularly in a changing conflict environment where conflicts are complex and interruptions are no longer short-term. Therefore interventions need to be linked with the process of conflict resolution to avoid health care or food aid being used by politically dominant groups.

Food Relief in Conflict Situations

Food interventions have both a survival and a production function. For example, food-for-work may be part of an income programme or food aid can be monetised to generate local currency. However, food aids have to be seen beyond the objective to fulfill nutritional goals, it also defines relationships between social groups in regard to food accessibility and how food is shared. Food aid is aiming to meet people's basic food requirements and minimising risk and severity of disease by complementing services such as basic health care.

In more stable political conditions where free food aid is given it presents an income transfer by releasing income, which normally is spent on food. However, in conflict situations food relief frequently becomes part of the dynamics of conflict such as in the case of Sudan where it is used to sustain the struggle between the North and the South without resolving it. Furthermore, the military attack food supplies in the fight against rebels who depend on the support from the communities.

Health is also a matter of food security. When food insecurity coincides with conflict situations, health and survival are threatened. Food security provided some concepts on how and why vulnerable households manage to survive in periods of hardship (coping strategies).

Coping Strategies in African Trouble Zones

Today, most conflicts in Africa such as the ones in the Great Lake Region, Angola or Congo cause major problems of food insecurity. They are linked to the civil wars which produce substantial social disruption as a result of massive population movements. The analysis of coping strategies showed that household respond to these conflict situation by eating less, selling livestock and land, or trying to find new sources of income.

In some emergency situations, however, such coping mechanisms may fall. In the case of the war in Mozambique food aid was vital since coping strategies were limited and people had to sell all their assets which was particular true for internationally displaced persons and refugees.

It has been argued that food relief bypasses local structures in favour of those qualifying on a nutrition status criterion, decided by international organisations, or it may attract populations to refugee camps to receive free food rations and thereby undermines local production. In the case of Rwanda food aid was targeted at the internally displaced and left out the local population. This can be due to donor bias in needs assessment.

Food scarcity is not always so result of civil war but its creation may be rather a political objective. An example is food relief manipulated by local elites and the military like in the case of Sudan. It can be summarised that generally relief operations often bear the risk of fueling the process of instability and violence rather than helping to contain the situation.

Lessons from Food Relief for the Health Sector

Through the experience of food relief in recent civil wars such as Sudan, Somalia, Mozambique etc., there has been an increasing awareness of the economic and political context in which operations takes place. Like food relief, health care is a political tool, which can, if not properly targeted, undermine peoples access to health care services. While food production is linked to food security, it is more difficult to identify factors leading to self-sufficiency in health care.

As mentioned above, food aid is aiming to insure survival. It also has an economic aspect, protecting household assets. Health care relief is targeted to assure immediate physical survival based on the importance of social health. Unfortunately, curative interventions hardly consider the socio-cultural dimension of health. Therefore it would be beneficial if health care interventions consider local norms and traditions. Interventions should be compatible and complement local health programmes. The emphasis should be on strengthening formal and non-formal health institutions both in service provision and training.

In food relief, distribution and needs assessment identification are controversial issues for discussion. While the programme design is shaped by donors perceptions, the actual programmes are influenced by the priorities of some powerful leaders as well as the socio-economic and political context.

Health care interventions need to analyses these issues in the context of economic and political systems in order to identify the most vulnerable groups, for example populations living in areas which are more, operations require a stronger involvement of communities both as users and active participants to carry out and maintain public health programmes.

There is a need for a new concept to be designed which applies to chronic emergencies. In the absence of a policy framework, guidelines need to be developed in order to overcome the inconsistency in planning and implementation. Donors need to change their assumptions on which they plan their health relief responses. A starting point in improving the efficiency of these operations is to provide institutional support to local authorities and organisations and involve them in the planning and implementation of programmes.

14

Environmental Protection

The Devil May Care

Back in the 1960s, most of us thought of the environment in terms of a medieval morality play. Thirty years later, those clear moral certainties are gone. Conservation has evolved into sustainable development (SD). And instead of denouncing the Devil of industry and all his works, the Goodies have become hopelessly ensnared in dialogue with him.

Most worrisome to all true believers, the debate between the SD movement and the private sector is proving remarkably fruitful. Indeed, this interface is the origin of many of the most interesting and provocative new ideas in sustainable development today.

The strategy for environmental protection in the 1970s relied overwhelmingly on government regulations and inspectors. Dubbed "Command-and-control" by business it involved government laying out detailed rules and using bureaucratic procedures to enforce them. Industry says that centralised hands-on regulation is inherently expensive and inefficient: the rules take so long to draw up that they impose standards that are two or more years out of date.

There are a number of reasons why command-and-control is no longer appropriate as a sole or primary strategy (except in some areas, such as nuclear power safety). Over the years, our concept of the proper role of the state has narrowed, with growing distaste for unnecessary bureaucratic control. And globalisation has created entirely new possibilities for market-based environmental management. A third reason is that the growth of civil society and its empowerment through the Internet have substantially increased the risks to business of egregiously bad environmental behaviour. In most countries, environmental stupidity by industry is now likely to be exposed, and public pressure is able to insist on expensive remedies.

However, one factor stands out above all: the rule-book approach to the environment is just too expensive. Even the rich industrialised countries can't afford more and more regulations, inspectors and control boards. And for the developing world, using scarce skilled workers as environmental police seems even less practical. The tendency now in the major industrialised countries is for government to set performance goals, and to let industry decide how to reach them.

You just can't trust these guys, right? But consider how we make companies keep more or less honest books. We don't have vast numbers of accountants on the public payroll counting through; the receipts of everyone from Exxon to the corner store. The state lays down the basic book-keeping rules, and makes every business pay for an independent auditor to make sure that the rules are obeyed. Classic self-regulation, at little cost to the taxpayer.

Why not do the same for pollution control, product and workplace safety? A raft of pilot schemes is now under way to do just that. For example, so far most self-regulating schemes lack transparency: they are not based on publicly available rules with published emissions levels. Nor are self-regulating companies usually accountable to anyone but themselves. These defects are recognised by some in industry, and attempts to correct them are being tested. So too is the concept of having such schemes formally registered with government, with legal or political sanctions for non-compliance.

Government likes self-regulation because it is cheap. And the SD lobby, somewhat unwillingly, is coming to accept this approach, especially for the developing world and "economies in transition". If Europe and North America couldn't afford command-and-control, how can countries with far fewer lawyers, administrators, chemical engineers and lab workers? Business says that self-regulation leaves the private sector alone to do what it does best: finding the most cost-effective ways of reaching agreed goals.

Not everyone in the SD camp is happy with this increasingly close relationship. Some environmentalists question the motives of business. But in the end, these are irrelevant. What really matter is what business does?

Business motives for SD are complex, and public relations is certainly one of them. Another is staff recruitment and morale: people don't like working for a company that is perceived to be damaging the environment. There are straight bottom-line motives too: bad environmental performance can depress stock prices and cause boardroom firings. It is cheaper to design a new plant for environmental standards of tomorrow than to engage in expensive retrofits later. And reducing waste has often proved extremely profitable.

Profit. The environment and development movements used to see this as a dirty word. But as these two groups melded into a single SD community, two key realisations started to emerge. The first was that sustainability does not ultimately depend on governments but on business, because business controls more than 90 per cent of the investment that shapes our future. The second was that business is based on profit so that achieving SD will require making sustainability profitable.

Making the profit motive work for sustainability is a carrot and stick affair—but without the stick the donkey would probably not go for the carrot.

In a competitive market, a boycott that cuts sales by a mere 10 per cent can make business hungry for the carrot.

One promising carrot is eco-labeling, which enables consumers to make positive SD choices. The problem is to get producers, retailers, campaigners and consumers to agree on who gets this green stamp of approval. What exactly is an energy-efficient light bulb, an organically grown pineapple or a sustainable logged armchair?

To someone reared on the view that you can't trust business at all sustainability initiatives seem to be cropping up In the oddest places. The world's insurance companies for example, are seriously worried about global warming, not just because it involves more storms, floods and severe weather, but because these events are unpredictable. Between 1991 and 1997, extreme weather cost in the insurance industry US $200 billion, and companies fear that further rapid climate change could cause widespread bankruptcies. As a result, insurance has been lobbying for tighter controls on carbon dioxide than those agreed to in Kyoto.

Business and sustainable development remain uneasy bedfellows. But what cannot be denied is that the interface between them is spawning a wealth of intriguing ideas, insights and approaches.

This does not mean that civil society, governments and international institutions should be doing whatever business wants. On the contrary, as the private sector grows beyond the power of all but the largest states, the need for governmental and inter-governmental ground rules and for grass roots and international analysis, monitoring and criticism is more urgent than ever. Market mechanisms and self-regulation are still in their infancy. But the pattern of government setting broad goals, and industry working out how to meet (or exceed) them, and being publicly accountable for doing so, will be centrally to SD in the 21st century.

****

15

Forests

The Earth's Lungs

The world's forest cover is shrinking. Over the past 50 years nearly half of the world's original forest cover has been lost—some 3 billion hectares. Each year another 16 million hectares of virgin forest are cut, bulldosed, or burned.

Between 1980 and 1995 the world lost some 180 million hectares of forest—an area the size of Indonesia. While developed countries had a net increase of 20 million hectares due to reforestation, this gain was more than offset by a net decrease of 200 million hectares in the developing world.

Forests have many functions of value both to humanity and to nature itself. Take away the trees, and the intricately linked ecosystem unravels. Forests absorb carbon dioxide and produce oxygen, anchor soils, regulate the water cycle, protect against erosion, and provide a habitat for millions of species.

Forest products are essential to the world economy, worth about US $400 billion annually in timber, pulp, paper, and fuel wood. Forest products other than wood, such as medicines, vegetables, and fruits, provide another US $20 billion and are growing in importance.

Healthy forests boost food production. Trees soak up and store water from season to season, slowly releasing moisture during dry periods. Without tree cover, water runs off faster during the tropical rainy season, carrying away valuable topsoil. A World Bank study found that the rate of soil loss was 10 times higher on forest lands where slash-and-burn shifting cultivation was practised than in undisturbed forests. One reason that agricultural yields have fallen in Sub-Sahran Africa is that vast amounts of forest cover have disappeared, hastening soil erosion and loss of soil nutrients.

Forest cover regulates climate, while destruction of forests contribute to global warming. Whereas living trees soak up and store carbon dioxide from the atmosphere trees that are cut down and burned release carbon into the atmosphere. In the last decade tropical deforestation has released large amounts of stored carbon—accounting for roughly one-quarter of the carbon dioxide emissions to the atmosphere due to human activity.

Pressures on Forests

Current demand for forests products may exceed the limits of sustainable consumption by 25 per cent. The developed world accounts for most of the demand for forest products. With just 16 per cent of the world's population, North America, Europe, and Japan consume two-thirds of the world's paper and paperboard and half its industrial wood. Demand for industrial wood products also has risen in developing countries, however, along with demand for fuel wood, the main energy source for many rural communities.

Throughout the 1990s many developing countries with rapid population growth had high rates of deforestation. Forest land was converted to agricultural use, and trees cut to provide housing and wood for fuel. Moreover developing countries stepped up exports of forests, products to meet the rising demand from developed countries.

The amount of forest area per capita fell by half between 1960 and 1995—reflecting both population growth and the disappearance of forest cover. In 1995 close to 1.7 billion people lived in countries with less than one-tenth of a hectare of forest cover per capita (83). By 2025, an estimated 4.6 billion people will live in such countries.

What can be Done?

As population grows and per capita consumption of forest products increases, countries must do more to manage forest resources on a sustainable basis. The following developments offer encouragement.

Technological Improvements: Technological improvements including use of recycled paper and paperboard, have substantially reduced the amount of pulp needed to produce paper. In 1970 paper and paperboard consisted of 80 per cent wood pulp. By 1997 more efficient production processes had reduced that figure to 56 per cent. As a direct result, the production of pulp for paper is expected to grow by just over 1 per cent a year over the next decade, about half the growth rate in the 1980s.

Forest Products Certification: Adopting a system that identifies forest products that come from sustainable managed forests could support efforts toward sustainability. As of 1998, about 10 million hectares of forest lands have been certified. Over 90 per cent of the certified area is in northern, temperature forests, mostly in Europe and North America. Close to 60 per cent of the entire certified area is in just two countries—Sweden and Poland—reflecting education and awareness campaigns in those countries. In tropical forests, where most of the destruction is taking place today, only tiny areas have been certified as providing sustainable yield.

Inter-governmental Responses: In 1995 the Inter-governmental Panel on Forests (IPF) was established in response to the 1992 Earth Summit. The IPF evolved into the inter governmental Forum on Forests in 1997, after the UN's five year review of the Earth Summit goals. The mission of the forum is to examine the underlying causes of deforestation and to help countries develop strategies that address them.

Efforts to advance an international legal convention on forests, which begin in 1990, have been shelved, however.

Some observers believe that advancing such a convention would only codify the standards of a weak consensus and thus would be worse than no convention at all. Widespread opposition to a convention makes it unlikely that the issues will reach the negotiating table.

Instead, many organisations urge governments of countries with large forest resources to enforce existing legislation and to introduce more effective forest conservation initiatives close to 130 countries have developed or updated their National Forest Programmes over the past decade.

While such initiatives are promising, they cannot be expected to half forest destruction completely. Millions of people rely on forest products for their livelihoods. Sustainable forest management will require not just enforcement of laws that project forests but also alternative sources of livelihood for many rural people.

****

16

The Environment, The Economy and Public Health

An Integrated View

The environment is central to the health of people and their economies. Just as a foetus is totally dependent on the life-support system of the mother during her pregnancy, so the health and vitality of people and their economies are totally dependent on their environments. Unfortunately, many people do not see it that way. They either see the environment as dependent on the economy—such as the politician who says: "let's make the economy strong, then we'll fix the environment when we can afford it"—or they see little connection between health and the environment, whether they are "deep greens" campaigning on ecological issues or doctors treating individual patients and individual illnesses. Whether we are politicians, greens or doctors, is there not a more efficient way to fulfil our aims? For this, a broader perspective is essential.

All economies are sub-systems of the larger environmental system which provides the:

- sources of energy and materials;
- sinks for pollution and other wastes;
- services of water, nutrients and carbon recycling;
- space for living, working and aesthetics ("a walk in the woods and the song of a bird").

Neglect of this life-support system of the "4 S's" leads to weaker or defunct economies as vegetation, food, soils, water or air become contaminated or exhausted and gradually fail to support economic activity. This is dramatically illustrated in the Aral Sea region, or the collapsed Canadian salmon fishing communities.

Indirect Social Costs

Less catastrophic but still costly is where economic damage is caused by pesticides and nutrient contamination of groundwater, involving millions of rupees in water treatment. This is a social cost to the economy that the agricultural sector does not include in the price of its food: an economic distortion that reduces the real wealth of society via false price signals that encourage the over-use of pesticides and fertilisers. Similarly, the "external" costs on society of road-respiratory-induced accidents, noise, respiratory and circulatory diseases and congestion amount to a lot of money to any government but these costs are not borne by transport users, which mean that transport is encouraged beyond the level that is economic for society as a whole. By internalising these externalities via taxes and other means, the market prices for transport would become fairer and more efficient. Currently only about 30 per cent of transport externalities are covered by transport taxes. But if the health of an economy is dependent on the health of its environment, what about the health of its people?

Without access to the basics of clean water, shelter, fresh air and food, people obviously suffer. Even in more developed economies where the link between everyday life and the environment is not so visible, the role of environmental factors in disease and well-being is significant. Most of the major diseases such as heart disease, cancer, respiratory diseases and allergies have an environmental as well as a genetic component within a multi-factorial chain of causation. And while each environmental factor may be small, if the links in the chain of causation are inter dependent, as they often appear to be then removing even a small link can break the chain.

Environmental Factors

Take asthma in children, for example. These seem to be many causes, from a child's genetic inheritance to its nutritional status, which in turn help determine how it reacts to the many environmental factors, both indoor (such as mites, pets, damp, environmental tobacco smoke, nitrogen oxides) and outdoor (such as pollen and pollution from industry and traffic), that have been implicated in asthma causation. Therefore it is clear that diagnoses of asthma and many other diseases should systematically embrace environmental factors. This will be a significant challenge for doctors whose time is scarce and whose training is not usually appropriate.

This multi-causal chain will vary in its exact make-up from child to child, but for children overall, even if the Evironmental factors such as damp housing to traffic fumes may be less important than, say, genetic make-up or nutritional status, the environmental factors may be the ones that can be most cost effectively removed, thus breaking the causal chain. And, as with many environmental issues, there are secondary benefits of action, such as less noise or fewer accidents from traffic reduction, or energy savings from dry houses, which further justify the environmental actions even where exact causations are not well understood.

The environmental causes of disease and ill-health are a controversial and ill-understood area of science and opinions vary about their significance. Some say that, for Western Europe, perhaps 2-3 per cent of public disease and ill-health is determined by known environmental factors but others maintain that it must be far more significant. They point to the sharp increase over the last two or three decades in asthma, allergies, and cancers (particularly of the reproductive organs such as breast and testicles) and related ill-health such as sperm count decline, which cannot be explained by genetic causes. They also observe that the large differences in health between the socio-economic classes cannot be explained without involving significant environmental causation.

It is thought that the ubiquitous presence of low doses of mixtures of chemicals in food, drink, air, consumer products and the general environment are playing some role in public ill-health, even if the evidence for this is far from substantial.

Impact on Public Health

But what about environmental programmes and campaigns being little concerned with health? Well, history so far shows that the environment only gets serious attention when it is seen to be damaging either the economy or public health. Yet because "everything connects" in "socio-enviro" systems, action to stop infectious diseases from water contamination, or to reduce skin cancer from ozone depletion, leads to a better environment for all species. And if upland forests are preserved because they are seen to be cheaper and more effective water regulators (which reduce the risk of lowland flooding) than dams, then upland biodiversity benefits anyway, even if it was last in the queue for political attention.

Although public health may be seen by some as only a small part of "the environment", much environmental progress depends upon the political weight of the health impacts. For example, the cost benefit exercise on the current multi-pollutant/effect programme on acidification, eutrophication and low-level ozone shows that it is the benefits to human health, not eco-system damage, that provide the main economic justification for further reductions in SO_2, NO_x and NH_3. Ecologists need the language of public health in order to maximise political support for the environment. So, it is out of our specialist "boxes" of economics, health and ecology, and into a shared systems approach, with integrated programmes that build partnerships for progress.

****

17

Population Growth and Climate Change

Over the last half-century, carbon emissions from fossil fuel burning expanded at nearly twice the rate of population, boosting atmospheric concentrations of carbon dioxide, the principal greenhouse gas, by 30 per cent over preindustrial levels. All major scientific bodies acknowledge the likelihood that climate change due to the build-up of greenhouse gases in the atmosphere is indeed under way. The 15 warmest years on record have all occurred since 1979 and 1998.

The destabilisation of our climate threatens more intense heat waves, more severe droughts and floods, more destructive storms, and more extensive forest fires. The related shifts in rainfall and temperature may jeopardize food production, the Earth's biological diversity, and entire ecosystems, as well as human health by expanding the ranges of tropical diseases. Unless efforts to curb them are stepped up, carbon emissions will continue to grow faster than population over the next 50 years, driving the Earth's climate system into unchartered territory. The Intergovernmental Panel on Climate Change (IPCC) estimates that an eventual two-thirds reduction in global emissions is needed to avoid precariously high levels of atmosphere carbon dioxide concentrations.

The IPCC and US Department of Energy (DOE) project that emissions from developing countries will nearly quadruple over the next half-century, while those from industrial nations will increase by 30 per cent. Although annual emissions from industrial countries are currently twice as high as from developing ones, the latter are on target to eclipse the industrial world by 2020.

Higher per capita carbon emissions accounts for roughly 55 per cent of the increase in emissions projected for developing nations. Emissions per person are due to more than double from 0.51 tons of carbon per year in 2000—just one-fifth of the industrial level—to 1.14 tons in 2050. The remaining 45 per cent of emissions increases is due to population growth.

Fossil fuel use accounts for roughly three quarters of world carbon emissions. As a result, regional growth in carbon emissions tend to occur where economic activity, and related energy use, is projected to grow most rapidly. Emissions in China are projected to grow over three times faster than population in the next half-century, as emissions per person soar from 0.77 tons of carbon to 2.81 tons due to booming economy that is heavily reliant on coal and other carbon-rich energy sources. In Africa, in contrast, emissions per person are expected to scarcely change-growing from the current level of 0.33 tons in 2050, despite a three-fold increase in total emissions.

The effects of population growth are most profound in countries where people are heavily emitters. For example, the 115 million people added to the population of the United States between 1950 and 1998—an increase of nearly 75 per cent in just 45 years—account for more than one-tenth of current global emissions. And the carbon emissions of the 75 million people who will be added to the US population in the next 50 years roughly equal the emissions of the 1.3 billion people who will be added to Africa during that period.

Deforestation and other landuse changes account for the remainder of world carbon emissions. Forests have served as a sink for carbon throughout much of human history. In recent years, however, the world's forests have become net sources of atmospheric carbon, largely due to forest burning and clearing in the tropics. Six months of fires in Asia in 1997 and 1998 released more carbon than Western Europe emits from fossil fuel burning in an entire year. The carbon contribution from this source will likely increase in coming years as the burgeoning human population continues to cut down forests.

18

Why Don't We Stop Tuberculosis?

Tuberculosis, a disease many people associate with sequestered sanatoriums that were long ago abandoned or rased, has now reemerged as the number one killer among the infectious or communicable diseases. The current TB epidemic is expected to grow worse, especially in India, because of the evolution of multi-drug-resistant strains and the emergence of AIDS, which compromises human immune systems and make them more susceptible to infectious diseases.

The resurgence of tuberculosis comes at a time when other infectious diseases that were once thought to be well-controlled—malaria and cholera, among them—have increased and new diseases, notably AIDS, have emerged. Despite the advances in modern medicine, infectious diseases have persisted and continue to have a major effect on public health; in the 50 years following the discovery of antibiotics, efforts to control age-old epidemics have been overcome not by a lack of medical knowledge but by structural problems, including the lack of adequate health care in many parts of India, and increased rates of travel and migration.

Tuberculosis has special characteristics that set it apart from other infectious diseases, most of which rely on mosquitoes, rats, or water to transmit infection. Tubercle bacilli only live in human tissues, and tuberculosis can only be transmitted by close contact with an infected person. In a healthy individual, the immune system is normally able to wall off and isolate the bacilli in a nodule. This essentially neutralizes the tubercle bacillus, so the person has what is referred to as an inert infection. If the immune system remains strong, there is only a 5 to 10 per cent chance of developing TB from an inert infection. But if the immune system is under severe stress—from HIV, diabetes, or chemotherapy for cancer, for example, the chances that the infection will develop into disease increase to as much as 10 per cent in a single year.

A person who has active TB can spread the infection simply by coughing, sneezing, singing, or even talking. Another person has only to inhale the bacilli to become infected. If the infection is not detected and treated promptly, one person with active tuberculosis can infect an average of 10 to 14 people in one year and sometimes many more.

Inert TB infections may show no symptoms at all. Only if those infections are activated these people will be at risk of developing the disease and transmitting it to others. Unfortunately, little is known about what activates a latent TB infection beyond the fact that people with healthy immune systems run a low risk of developing an active case of TB.

Because the already poor and disenfranchised Indian population carry a disproportionate burden of tuberculosis, the disease has a certain stigma attached to it. But the unsanitary and crowded living conditions that are often connected to poverty do not cause TB to spread; they increase the chances that the infection will spread from person to person and the chances that a person's immune system may already be weak and therefore less able to fight the infection. Despite the misconceptions, tuberculosis is exacerbated only by the failure to detect and treat the infection properly and by close contact with infected individuals.

More than 95 per cent of TB cases reported in 1995 were in the developing world, an estimated two-thirds of them in Asia. India accounted for 2.1 million cases. India is with a disproportionate number of cases because AIDS is spreading quickly, health services are inadequate, and little money is available for treatment.

To identify and diagnose TB must be combined with sufficient infrastructure and resources, such as vaccines, medicines, trained health personnel, and clinics. As with other diseases, funding for research and prevention and treatment programmes is essential. Thanks to modern medicine, there is a low-cost, effective TB treatment with high cure rates among infected adult. But if patients don't take the drugs consistently or don't complete treatment, TB strains develop that are more resistant to medicine, and sometimes even untreatable. If this drug regimen were used throughout India. It would reduce the rate of transmission and cut the number of deaths by half over the next 10 years.

The growing TB epidemic is a classic case of a public health crisis in India that could be headed off easily and inexpensively. Its fate will largely depend on the willingness of government and public health officials to invest up front in prevention and early intervention. If we ignore the extraordinary opportunity that exists now to fight the epidemic, we will pay a high price in lives and extensive health care costs later.

19

Action for Safe Motherhood

Countries vary enormously in terms of the situations and challenges they face and their capacity to address these. However, experience from around the world over the past decade has demonstrated that a number of features are common to successful efforts to address maternal mortality. Reducing maternal mortality requires coordinated, long-term efforts. Actions are needed within families and communities, in society as a whole, in health systems, and at the level of national legislation and policy. Further, interactions among the interventions in these areas are critical to reducing maternal mortality and to building and supporting momentum for change.

Legislative and Policy Actions

Changes in legislation and policy are essential to ensure safe motherhood. Long-term political commitment is an essential prerequisite. When decision-makers at the highest levels are resolved to address maternal mortality, the resources needed will be mobilised and the essential policy decisions will be taken. Without this level of commitment over the long-term, projects cannot become programmes and activities cannot be sustained.

A supportive social, economic, and legislative environment allows women to overcome the various obstacles that limit their access to health care, such as distance from their homes to appropriate health facilities, lack of transport and, more critically, financial and social barriers. Proper maternal health care is limited when women have to pay for services and essential drugs, and when they must bear substantial hidden costs such as time lost for housework, paid employment, food production, and child care. Legislation that supports women's access to care must be formulated to permit health workers at the periphery of the health system to perform specific life-saving functions. Failing this, only highly skilled health professionals, based largely in urban centres, can provide such care, and only women with sufficient money and the means to reach such centres can benefit from it.

With these objectives, careful review of national laws and policies is necessary, particularly in the following areas:

- ***Family Planning:*** Statutes that restrict women's access to family planning services (e.g. by requiring that a woman be married or that she should have her husband's approval) should be repealed. Policies must ensure that all couples and individuals have access to good-quality, voluntary, client-oriented, and confidential family planning information and to services that offer a wide choice of effective contraceptive methods. Policies should address regulatory, social, economic, and cultural factors that limit women's control over sexuality and reproduction, in order that pregnancies that are too early, too late, or too frequent may be avoided.
- ***Adolescents and Children:*** Policies and programmes should encourage late marriage and childbearing and an expansion of the economic and educational opportunities for girls and women. Promotion of good nutrition in childhood and adolescence, as well as supplementation if necessary during pregnancy, provides protection for both women and their future children. Policies should also enable adolescents to take responsibility for and protect their sexual and reproductive health, and facilitate their access to health information and services. All children, before they reach the age at which they become sexually active, need to

be taught the risks of unprotected sex and helped to develop the skills needed to protect themselves from sexual coercion.

- ***Barriers to Access:*** Assigning health workers trained in midwifery to village-based health facilities can help over-come problems of distance and transport. Health workers should also be trained to deal sympathetically with women patients. Policies should support the provision of services at minimum cost, at the same time, health workers should have job security, be paid adequate wages, and be provided with sufficient supplies to do their jobs. Policies that will increase women's decision-making power, particularly in regard to their own health, are also essential.
- ***Regulation of Practice:*** Protocols and statutes aimed at providing both routine maternal care and referral facilities for obstetric complications at each level of the health system need to be developed. Responsibilities at each level for supervision, deployment of health care personnel, remuneration, and reporting procedures must be defined nationally. Development and promotion of education and training curricula are important, as is the setting of national norms and standards to govern the selection of trainees, trainers, and supervisors.
- ***Delegation of Authority:*** Services should be decentralised so that facilities are available as close to people's homes as possible. Adequate supplies and equipment and trained staff should be available in all health facilities, particularly in rural and remote areas, together with written policies and protocols to guide service provision and to allow certain functions to be delegated to personnel at lower levels (when appropriately trained).
- ***Abortion:*** Availability of services for management of abortion complications and post-abortion care should be ensured by appropriate legislation. Where abortion is

not prohibited by law, facilities for the safe termination of pregnancy should be made available. National policy can discourage unsafe abortion practices by promoting protection against unwanted pregnancy, and national helath campaigns to publicize the risks of unsafe abortion and the need to recognize and seek treatment for abortion complications.

20

AIDS and the Responsibility of the Media

HIV/AIDS is one of the most terrible diseases the world has ever known. Estimates are that 37 million people worldwide are already infected with the deadly virus which weakens the human immunity system and leaves the body unprotected for the onslaught of a host of other diseases. So far, there is no vaccine to shield people against HIV and there is no effective cure for the disease. This means that people inevitably die once they have caught the virus although some ten years or more may pass before the actual outbreak of AIDS in its final stages. UN figures say that 23 million of HIV/AIDS infected people live in Sub-Saharan Africa alone, and all of them are doomed to die a painful death. At least 4 million newly infected were added to that number every year. As a result of the epidemic, life expectancy on the continent, which had been climbing persistently during the first three decades of post-independence development, will drop by ten years and more in many countries, especially in Southern Africa. And it will be the young, economically active people—who are also the sexually most active ones—that will be prominent among the victims. AIDS thus is not only a humanitarian disaster, it is also threatening to become another source of economic retardation and backwardness.

Why then there is still so little attention paid to the looming cirsis? Why are African leaders not getting together to discuss what needs to be done to control the situation? Why are they not using every means at their disposal to hammer the message home to their people: AIDS can be reigned in through more responsible behaviour and a change in sexual practices?

In Europe and America, when AIDS surfaced as a common threat in the late 1980s, every effort was made to alarm the public and especially the most vulnerable groups homosexuals, sex workers, people with frequently changing sex partners—about the dangers of unprotected sex. It was especially through the media that the almost everybody became aware of the AIDS menace. Prominent individuals—film stars, pop musicians, artists—who had been infected with AIDS outed themselves in the media and used their fame in anti-AIDS campaigns. Existing taboos on sexual practices were deliberately broken, and safer sex became a publicly debated issue. Much emphasis was placed on using condoms as a cheap and simple, but usually effective means to avoid infection. As a result of the public awareness campaigns and the continuous media coverage, new HIV infections in industrial countries returned to a relatively low level, and the disease today is considered to be under control, even though no medical cure has yet been found to treat AIDS patients.

While these successes were achieved in developed countries, the disease has been spreading with increasing speed in Africa and, lately, in Asia. Here, the society has reacted with far less openness to the challenges posed by AIDS. For a long time, political leaders and the media negated the menace in the erroneous belief that AIDS was mainly a disease of the decadent west. When they woke up to fact that AIDS was a problem not only for homosexuals in Los Angeles, London, or Berlin but also for "normal" heterosexual men and women in Uganda, South Africa or India, sexual taboos and religious inhibitions as well as social customs and attitudes proved powerful obstacles to launching publicity campaigns on the model of the Western countries.

As a result, there is still far too little information in developing countries on AIDS as a disease and what people can do to protect themselves against it. A recent study published by Johns Hopkins university in the United States, for instance, shows that only between 5 and 33 per cent of unmarried men are using condoms in sexual intercourse to avoid infection with AIDS. With women, condoms are even less known or popular than with men. The study says that the number of couples using condoms regularly is still very low worldwide. Instead of the 6 to 9 billion condoms used at present, 24 billions are required to control new infections. This is a question of money, because many of the people who ought to use condoms are among the poorest groups in breaking down barriers created out of prejudice and ingrained sexual behaviour.

Here, the media have a vital role to play. It is not enough to put up a few posters in town which warn against AIDS. The message has to be direct and concrete—Mechai in Thailand has shown how a witty and effective pro-condom campaign can be conducted even in a country with a strong Buddhist tradition—and it should not shy away from breaking sexual taboos. Equally important all media should be used—newspapers, radio, TV, films, video—to carry the message. AIDS awareness should always be part of reproductive health information, and needed, both are part of the same coin: if more condoms are used to prevent unwanted pregnancies, a welcome side-effect will be a reduction in new HIV infections.

AIDS and the menace it poses to the survival of large parts of African and Asian populations is not a pleasant subject. But it will not go away by keeping silent about its threat. Political leaders and the media must make it a topic for urgent action. And the people must change their sexual habits and behaviour and opt for safer sex. Otherwise, the future of whole regions on this globe will be grim.

* * * *

21

Children's Health and the Environment

Children today live in an environment vastly different from that of a few generations ago. Economic development, increased urbanisation and the consequences of war in many countries have added to the traditional environmental hazards, those problems associated with environmental pollution. Thus, while some traditional children's diseases such as diarrheoa, malnutrition and infectious diseases persist in many countries, environmentally-related illnesses such as asthma, respiratory illnesses due to environmental tobacco smoke (ETS), as well as mortality and morbidity due to injuries, are increasing. In childhood cancer in some countries and the potential risks of endocrine-disrupting chemicals are among the emerging health threats that need careful vigilance. Children of lower socio-economic status are likely to suffer disproportionately from all these health threats as a consequence of living in highly polluted environments, poor quality housing, lower levels of education, and of restricted access to environmental and health care services.

Children's Vulnerability

The concern for children's vulnerability to environmental health threats is based on several factors. Children receive greater exposures than adults do because they drink more water, eat more food and have higher breathing rates per unit of body weight. Because they are undergoing rapid growth and development, toxicant effects at specific times may have irreversible consequences. For example, if vital connections between nerve cells fail to form during brain development, there is high risk that the resulting neuro-behavioural dysfunction will be permanent and irreversible. Also, because most children have more future year of life than adults, they have more time to develop any chronic disease that may be triggered by early environmental exposures.

Public Health Threats

Asthma, injuries, and the effects of Environmental Tobacco Smoke (ETS) are among the most significant public health threats to children. Childhood asthma is increasingly prevalent in almost all countries. What causes asthma is not known, but several environmental factors, such as indoor air quality (particularly exposure to the house-dust mite) and ETS, have been linked with the increase in asthma. In addition, outdoor air pollutants such as particulates; sulphur dioxide and ozone can exacerbate asthma symptoms. ETS, especially smoking by the mother, is a known risk factor for asthma. ETS is also known to cause acute and chronic middle ear disease and is associated with sudden infant death syndrome (SIDS).

Potential for Prevention

The variation in asthma and injury rates and the evidence of the role of certain environmental factors underline the potential for prevention. Public policies should seek to avoid preventable childhood diseases by preventing exposures to environmental agents and considering children's characteristics and susceptibilities in the development of environmental health legislation. Promoting citizen awareness and participation in policy-making through education and access to environmental information are important elements in achieving a safe environment for children. In this context, children are not only consumers with rights, but also citizens who can play an active role towards their own protection.

International Awareness

Several international agreements have acknowledged

children's vulnerabilities and have committed their signatories to protect children's health from the effects of a deteriorating environment. This year, many countries will address several of the environmental health threats to children through international and national action. It is expected that a large international collaborative initiative will result under the guidance of WHO and other international organisations.

22

Taking Poverty to Heart

Non-Communicable Diseases and the Poor

Non-Communicable Diseases (NCDs) are the leading cause of death worldwide. Their emergence as the predominant health problem in wealthy countries accompanied economic development. As a result, NCDs are often referred to as 'diseases of affluence'. But is this a misleading term? It suggests that these are not major problems for the world's poor, which is quite simply wrong, as this article illustrates. Is it time to rethink policy on NCDs?

NCDs include cardiovascular disease (CVD), such as stroke and heart attack, diabetes, chronic lung disease, cancer, diseases of bones and joints and mental illness. The single biggest killer is coronary heart disease, followed by other CVDs, cancer and chronic lung disease. Diabetes is a major contributor to deaths from CVD, but also causes its own unique complications. Common risk factors for these conditions include smoking, physical activity, obesity and diets high in saturated fat and sodium and low in fruit and vegetables.

By 2020, NCDs will be the biggest cause of death in all regions apart from Sub-Saharan Africa. It is predicted that in 2010, the number of people with diabetes worldwide will be double the level in 1995 and that the biggest increase (both proportionately and in absolute number) will be in poorer regions. CVD occurs at an earlier age in developing countries, increasing the potential adverse economic and social consequences.

NCDs are already major health problems for adults in the poorest countries of the world. Demographic data show that age-specific death rates from NCDs in Tanzania are higher than in wealthier countries. Mortality rates for some NCDs, such as stroke, are particularly high. However, while NCDs account for 80 per cent of adult deaths in developed regions, the figure is less than 30 per cent in Tanzania, reflecting the continuing burden of infectious disease. Countries like Tanzania suffer the 'worst of both worlds'. Even within a country, 'diseases of affluence' is a misleading term. A more accurate label is 'diseases of Urbanisation'. Several studies from developing countries show increased levels of high blood pressure and other NCD risk factors in urban compared to rural populations. Even within urban areas, the more affluent do not always suffer the greatest burden.

The rise of NCDs in developing countries is inextricably linked to economic and cultural globalisation. This is exemplified by the activities of multinational tobacco companies. Tobacco-related deaths will exceed the toll due to HIV and become the single largest preventable cause of death by 2020. Curbing the effects of globalisation on the prevention and treatment of NCDs will also require regulation of food and agriculture multinationals and the pharmaceutical and health care industries.

Much of the projected rise in NCDs is preventable, particularly that due to smoking, poor diet, physical inactivity and obesity. Early action in some populations could prevent the emergence of these risk factors altogether; in other, the challenge is to reduce established levels. Although it is unclear whether all major risk factors are equally important in every region, the strength and consistency of data on the core risk factors in several ethnic groups justify preventative action now.

Lessons from risk factor intervention studies in rich and middle income countries suggest that success requires:

- Broad intersectoral action;
- Community participation;
- Appropriate legislation;
- Involvement of appropriate NGOs;
- Health services changes—to manage those at high risk and promote public education.

Even apparently minor changes, such as a small fall in average population blood pressure, can have substantial benefits. However, some preventative programmes have produced disappointing results and almost all have failed to halt the ubiquitous increase in obesity. This highlights the difficulty of promoting healthy behaviour by individuals who are surrounded by barriers to change and inducements to lead an unhealthy lifestyle.

Health systems in developing countries face both a growing need for prevention programmes and increasing numbers of individuals requiring treatment. The complications of high blood pressure and diabetes can be reduced by the delivery of effective health care. Crucially, this entails:

- Partnership between patients and health professionals with the knowledge, ability and resources to take appropriate measures over many years;
- Cheap and effective drugs and the implementation of simple treatment protocols, as promoted by WHO and the CVD initiative of the Global Forum for Health Research.

An appropriate policy and strategic framework is essential for such initiatives to be effective on a large scale. Even in the poorest countries people are already seeking health care for NCDs in both the public and private sectors, particularly in urban areas. Whatever the balance of priorities between different conditions, existing resources should be used as effectively as possible. Rapid evaluation methods can provide policy-makers with information on the current levels and quality of care and identify the main opportunities for improving health services.

The proper planning and co-ordination of NCD prevention and treatment, whether globally or nationally, requires up-to-date data on risk factor and disease levels—currently missing for much of the world. To address this lack, the WHO Non-Communicable Disease and Mental Health Surveillance section is promoting a standardised approach to enable comparisons across regions and over time, preparing the first ever 'world risk status' report for the major NCDs. This will provide a truly global perspective on the size and nature of the problem.

As this article has shown, NCDs are major health problems even in the world's poorest countries, including those regions where infectious diseases continue to take a huge toll. The NCD burden will grow substantially in low land middle-income countries over the next 10 to 20 years. NCDs will increasingly demand attention and require the right balance between competing priorities for prevention, cure and care. In meeting this challenge, national policy-makers will need to follow the lead of WHO and develop a strategic framework that plans for surveillance, prevention and appropriate health sector reforms.

* * * *

23

Energy and Sustainability

Mankind's history is marked by a growing use of energy which until the end of the Industrial Revolution came largely from renewable sources. It was coal that fed the furnaces and boilers of the Industrial Revolution from the end of the seventeenth century to the nineteenth century, and drove railway transport and steamships. As well as being a useful source of mechanical energy, it was also used in the manufacture of coal gas for street lighting and in the chemical industry. In fact, coal was the principal form of energy until 1900.

Discoveries at the beginning of the nineteenth century allowed the use of electricity and revealed the relations and the interconvertibility of different forms of energy. The principles of conservation and of energy quality did not become operative until much later. Meanwhile, in 1882, the first system for producing and distributing electricity in a large city was installed. This was the beginning of the second phase in industrialisation through electrification.

Following the first successful oil drillings in 1859, Standard Oil, the first of the modern large scale oil companies, attempted the first vertical structure for overall control of the oil process. It involved extraction from the subsoil, storage, refining and final distribution. Later, the growth of derivatives, the lower extraction costs compared to coal and the greater ease and economy of transport made oil modern society's basic energy source.

The internal combustion engine led to motorisation on a massive scale by land, sea and air and guaranteed a constantly growing market for petrol. The forties marked the start of the new petrochemical industry, which gave rise to an enormous number of new products; synthetic rubber, plastic, medicines, cosmetics, varnishes, artificial fibres, detergents, weedkillers, fertilizers, butane, propane, etc., opening the way to the mass-production of consumer goods and introducing new, non-biodegradable substances into the environment.

After World War II, ambitious programmes to produce electricity from nuclear energy were begun, in the search for a return on the enormous amounts of money invested. The economic expansion in the West during the fifties and sixties was directly related to enormous petrol consumption at a time when energy was considered plentiful and cheap. Energy consumption during these decades grew more than exponentially. The fastest developing industrial sectors were precisely the ones that consumed most energy—petrochemical industries, metallurgy, car manufacturing, domestic appliances, electricity generating, etc.—and a trend developed towards goods and services with higher energy intensity. Since 1950, increased energy production has been systematically favoured over more rational use. So much so that the increase in energy consumption has been taken as a reliable indicator of progress.

The Aftermath of the Oil Boom

The oil crises of 1973 and 1980 showed up the fragility of an energy system that was over-dependent on oil. The War in the Gulf was reminder of what was at stake for the Western economies; free access to cheap oil in the Middle East. It was therefore fear of the hardship caused by the first crisis that brought about a change in attitudes in Western countries; efforts were directed at breaking free from this dependence, diversifying supply sources, perfecting replacement energies and promoting energy-saving programmes.

The eighties marked a change in people's awareness about environmental problems. The damage was making itself felt in more and more places and eventually the global threat to our planet as a result of our energy system became clear; the composition of the atmosphere was changing and could lead to possible changes in the climate.

According to recent figures, 82 per cent of all the energy consumed in the world is produced by burning fossil fuels, 7.5 per cent from burning biomass, 5.5 per cent from the use of hydraulic energy and 5 per cent from nuclear energy. Most of our energy in other words, in non-renewable; it runs out as we use it, as the population increases; and it comes from fossil fuels, which on burning increase the amount of CO_2 in the atmosphere. If we add to this the accumulation of nuclear waste, the problems of access to oil deposits, constant spillages during transport and all the different imbalances involved in the world energy system, the outlook is far from sustainable.

The inequalities speak for themselves; globally, less than a quarter of the world's richest population consumes almost three quarters of the energy commercialised in the world. For example, the average annual consumption per capita in the United States is 26 times higher than in India.

The Choice of Change

Opening the way to societies that make sustainable use of energy necessarily involves increasing and improving energy efficiency, both in supply technologies and in end-use technologies, at the same time using renewable energy sources instead of fossil fuels.

Choosing the right system for the transformation of primary energy sources into energy services such as lighting, cooling, cooking, mechanical force, transport, etc. and choosing the most suitable appliances and technologies in each case is fundamental.

The truth is that a good standard of living is possible without wasting anything like as much energy. A series of relatively straightforward measures today allow a far higher level of comfort than in 1950, using one-third as much energy for heating water for washing in the home.

Petrol consumption by vehicles has dropped by 40 per cent in forty years, from 8 litres/100 kilometres to 5.3 litres in some models, and the work of improving their energy efficiency continues. In industry, the energy consumption necessary for manufacturing large intermediary products (steel, cement, paper or fertilizer) is decreasing steadily at a rate which varies between 0.5 per cent and 0.2 per cent per year according to the product.

Today's incandescent bulbs consume one twentieth as much electricity as bulbs in the twenties. The compact fluorescent bulbs now available can cut this down again to one-fifth. Efficiency in lighting has increased one-hundredfold. The use of new materials and a more rational use of traditional materials allows a reduction in the amount of energy and raw materials consumed. Building a house, for example, requires 20 per cent less energy than in 1950; building a vehicle, 40 per cent less. On a global level, reducing our society's energy-intensiveness is the first step towards energy sustainability.

24

Population Growth and Energy

It has been scarcely 200 years—the dawn of the Industrial Revolution—since humans abandoned sole reliance on firewood, other biomass fuels, and direct sunlight to meet daily energy needs. In the past half-century, global demand for energy grew twice as fast as population, as industrial nations burned coal, oil and natural gas to fuel their economies. Over the next half-century, world energy demands are projected to continue expanding beyond population growth, as developing countries try to catch up with industrial nations.

Developing countries will see tremendous growth in energy consumption in the next half-century, as growing populations and increasing affluence combine to drive their energy demands to dizzying levels. Based on projections from the US Department of Energy and the Intergovernmental Panel on Climate Change, total energy consumption in the developing world will grow by 336 per cent—nearly three times faster than population—over the next 50 years, from 3,499 million tons of oil equivalent to 15,255 million tons. By 2030, energy consumption in the developing world will likely surpass usage in industrial nations.

Rising per capita consumption accounts for nearly two-thirds of the growth in energy demand in poorer nations, but different population trajectories can have dramatic effects on future demands. For example, assuming the same growth in per capita energy demand, moving to the low UN population projection will reduce total energy demands from developing countries by 2,792 million tons of oil equivalent the output of nearly 3,000 average-sized coal-fired power plants.

In the next 50 years, the greatest growth in energy demands will come where economic activity is projected to be highest: In Asia, where consumption is expected to grow 361 per cent, though population will grow by just 50 per cent. Energy consumption in Latin America and Africa is projected to increase by 340 per cent and 326 per cent, respectively. Lower rates of population growth in Asia, compared with Latin America and Africa, mean that energy use per person will increase most in Asia. Nonetheless, in all three regions, local pressures on energy sources, ranging from forests to fossil fuel reserves to waterways, will be significant.

When per capita energy consumption is high, even a low rate of population growth can have significant effect on total energy demand. In the United States, for example, where current per capita energy demand is nearly double that in other industrial nations and over 13 times that in developing countries, the 75 million people projected to be added in the next 50 years will boost energy demands by 758 million tons of oil equivalent, roughly the same as the present energy consumption of Africa and Latin America.

World energy use per person doubled between 1950 and 1973, before confronting a short-term slowdown when restricted exports from oil-producing nations drove up energy prices. Another price shock, combined with a global economic recession, resulted in the slowdown of the early 1980s. The most recent stumbling block in energy growth followed the 1989 revolution in Eastern Europe, when energy use in the former Soviet states plummeted. Although DOE and IPCC project substantial future growth, similar forces may act to check such a development.

World oil production per person reached a high in 1979 and has since declined 23 per cent. Moreover, estimates of when global oil production will peak range from 2011 by petro-consultants to 2025 by the IPCC, signaling future price shock as long as oil remains the world's dominant fuel. Although people born in 1950 saw per capita oil production quickly double in a few short decades, those born in 2000 are likely to see it cut in half, dropping below 1950 levels.

In addition, meeting increased energy demands will require more storage and transportation infrastructure. Communities without a reliable supply of clean water or an adequate system for waste disposal may also fall short in connection to power supplies. For the estimated 2 billion who are still off the grid, and also experiencing high rates of population growth, decentralised energy technologies, such as solar roof shingles and fuel cell power generators, are likely the most feasible and affordable option for meeting increased energy demands.

Yet it will not necessarily be the scarcity of fuel that constrains future growth in energy consumption, but rather concerns about climate change, air quality and water quality. Growing climate concerns will require massive reductions in fossil fuel use at a time when demand for energy is soaring. A shift to renewable energy sources, such as solar energy and wind power, in addition to continued efficiency gains for power plants, cars and appliances, holds great promise for meeting future energy demands without adverse ecological consequences.

* * * *

25

Economics and Environment

Statistics change our view of the world. So statistics, however objective and accurate, are never value free but focus on what societies deem important. For better or worse, they guide government, business and individual decisions.

Until recently, the old game of India's economic growth was unquestioned and the score was kept between the national players by comparing their Gross National Product (GNP) or its narrower domestic version, Gross Domestic Product (GDP). It is time to take a closer look at the proliferation of new scoreboards, statistics and quality-of-life indexes which will redefine wealth and progress and change the future direction of human society.

Clarifying Values

These new scorecards and the 'greening' of GNP/GDP national accounts reflect the new 'green' accounting in thousands of balance sheets, reports and books on environment. At the very least, assumptions underlying old and new indicators are being clarified. The debate is still over what rather than how to measure, and what to do about values and amenities that are priceless.

The costs of GNP growth are now obvious—from felled forests, pollution exhausted soils, depleted natural resources and holes in the ozone layer to disrupted cultures and communities.

The concept of GNP/GDP was adapted into national accounting in India. With little re-examination, it continues to value bombs and bullets (defence expenditure), highly while setting the values of defence expenditure, education and public infrastructure—not to mention clean air and water and other environmental assets—at zero. It also ignores the some 50 per cent of production, which is unpaid—such as do-it-yourself home construction and repairs, food growing, household maintenance, parenting children and volunteering. In India such unpaid work can comprise up to 75 per cent of all production, particularly in agriculture sector.

Systems of National Accounts are based on GNP/GDP. Few economists, trade negotiators or development agencies questioned the basic assumption underlying it: that economies were generally in equilibrium, and that adding up a society's production and exchange of goods and services, measured in money terms, defined wealth and progress—however many social and environmental 'bads' came along with the 'goods'. Today's debates concern how best to calculate the costs of these 'bads' of production passed on to taxpayers or future generations. Some are easy to quantify: Costs of cleaning up pollution can be calculated, and their increase marches in lock-step with the expansion of pollution control and environment industry sectors.

Confusing means with ends: Indian Government officials, business executives, academics and hundreds of thousands of civic organisations are beginning to agree that we have been confusing means (i.e. GNP growth) with ends (human development and the survival and further evolution of our species under drastically changed planetary conditions).

New environmental and resource realities, legislation and insurance liabilities are driving further overhauling of traditional accounts. There is a big issue over whether new indicators will be weighted in money terms to expand GDP, or whether the separate components—health, education, environment, etc.—should be 'unbundled' so that the public can follow their own concern and hold politicians accountable for results:

Macro-economists still try to expand GDP by pricing environmental amenities and costs. Social and natural scientists, while agreeing that environmental amenities must be valued at more than zero in GDP, advocate 'unbundled' physical indicators, such as water and air quality measures and rates of infant mortality. They suspect that economists 'contingent prices' for valuing the environment are theoretical and arbitrary.

Such 'Shadow prices' are derived by ecomomists from historic welfare theories and formulas based on 'willingness to pay' (WTP) of willingness to be compensated'. Thus, to arrive at a price for valuing a marshland (one of the most productive ecosystems on the planet), economists could poll voters and residents with no motives other than appreciation for marshes and their non-monetary or aesthetic values or their desire to preserve them and the rare species they might contain. Such contingent prices would be lower than those offered by a hotel developer with profit motives or by a biotechnology firm which had identified species in the area that could be used for pharmaceutical products. Worse, such pricing discounts poor people's needs and concerns, since they cannot afford to participate. Here the price system should be subordinated to more democratic decision-making, such as voting on whether or not to protect the marsh.

Economic Accountability

Most social and natural scientists, as well as voters, believe that economics must now take its place within interdisciplinary teams of statisticians from health, education, energy and environmental policy fields. Economics is not a science by rigorous standards, but a profession often lacking in the quality assurances and accountability that governs lawyers and doctors. GNP is a malfunctioning strand of our 'cultural DNA code'—carrying erroneous information and signalling to the body-politic a form of growth analogous to that of cancer cells which consume the host's body. The new national accounting methods being redesigned to correct or even replace GNP/GDP will function like healthy 'cultural DNA strands', newly spliced in to govern healthier growth and more normal development patterns for human societies. Quantitative growth is dominant as children grow to adulthood, but once their mature size and weight are reached, this gives way to qualitative growth: education, social skills, broader awareness and even greater ethical understanding and wisdom. The statistical shift from GNP/GDP to sustainable development indicators mirrors such maturing of societies, recognising new goals and the traits human beings must now rapidly develop if we are to restructure our society for sustainability.

The new scorecards allow Indians to move beyond economism and ideologies of left and right to measure results directly and hold our business and government leaders accountable for implementing progress on the major goals of individual voters, consumers and investors. The new scorecards can help broaden trade pacts to include sustainable development criteria.

****

26

Water Problem in South India

Southern India's fast-growing urban areas and its farmers will collide over water allocation unless the government and water users take swift action. Urgently needed are measures that ensure efficient water use in cities and on farms, including regulation of groundwater withdrawal, restoration of traditional rain-collecting reservoirs, and experimentation with different cropping strategies.

In India's arid southern tip, typifies the plight of the country's extensive drylands. Scanty rainfall means residents often must get by on water drawn from small reservoirs and underground sources.

Extended dry periods are punctuated by intense monsoon bursts. When rains lash South India during the monsoons, only a fraction of the downpour is captured for later use. The rivers are seasonal and small compared to the Himalayan cataracts up north.

During the monsoon, these waters swell briefly to gigantic proportions recharging the water tables in their basins and then subside. In times of drought, when the rivers are narrow ribbons, water drawn from below ground sustains crops.

In the cities of South India the problems of water supply are exacerbated by antiquated or nonexistent infrastructures that cannot keep up frentic growth.

Farmers in South India depend on irrigation to see them through the growing season. They draw their water from three sources: Government canals that bring water from rivers and dams, traditional reservoirs known as "Tanks", and public and private wells often fitted with electric pumps. All three need to be made more efficient.

Besides being enormously expensive, large surface irrigation canals and dams are plagued by massive leaking and evaporation. Tanks collect rain water runoff behind small earthen dams. But these are falling into disrepair as farmers take advantage of low interest government loans and heavily subsidised electricity to switch to private wells fitted with electric pumps. Without maintenance, the tanks fill up with silt and hold less water.

As more wells are dug and as percolation tanks that once recharged underground water supplies fall into disuse, the water table is dropping at a rapid rate. Farmers who can afford to install powerful electric or diesel pumps on their wells are able to tap the retreating water table, but poorer farmers who raise their water by hand or cattle power from shallow wells often come up dry.

No regulations govern the amount of water a farmer can withdraw from a well, so underground reserves are available on a first-come, first-served basis. Add to this situation electricity rates based on the horsepower of pumps, not on the amount of electricity they consume, and there's no incentive to save water.

Any effort to limit groundwater extraction carries heavy political liabilities. Politicians are reluctant to risk raising thereof farmers, who provide the majority of their votes.

Preventing overdraft where water tables are falling would be a first step toward correcting water troubles. While some areas face the prospect of rationing, others have an abundance of groundwater still to be tapped. Effective legislation must be based on detailed and accurate map of groundwater supplies—something that doesn't currently exist.

They should also consider instituting higher user fees for its public canal projects and retuning to its old policy of charging farmers according to the electricity they consume. Making farmers pay closer to the full price for water and electricity would provide revenue for digging communal wells equipped with electric pumps and overhauling the tank system, while providing an incentive for farmers to conserve.

Using tanks and wells together maximizes the effectiveness of both, since tanks take pressure of groundwater supplies and wells sustain crops during their final weeks of growth when tanks are low. Any efforts to limit the number of new wells dug has to include measures that provide something to those without water, otherwise only those who currently own wells will benefit from groundwater conservation.

Officials might also experiment with encouraging farmers to plant less water-demanding crops such as ragi, sorghum and pulses in place of cotton, sugarcane, bananas and spices.

If politicians act now, they still have a chance to craft measures that are fair rather than desperate. The time is nearing water for drinking and irrigating crops will have to be called from careful conservation rather than from the ground.

* * * *

27

Water

An Educational and Informative Approach

The most characteristic element of our planet is undoubtedly water. Indeed, more than two-thirds of the earth's surface is covered by water—the total volume representing almost 1,500 million cubic kilometers. About 94 per cent of this water is found in the oceans, almost 6 per cent is located underground and in glaciers whereas rivers, lakes, soil moisture and atmospheric vapour, which constitute the major source of drinking water, account for a mere 0.0221 per cent of the total volume.

Water is indispensable for all living organisms. Life, as we know it, is impossible without water. It is present in all aspects of our life—directly or indirectly next to the air we breathe and together with the soil that we live upon, water constitutes the most important part of our environment, our most precious resource. And yet, except in the arid or semi-arid regions of the world, its value is generally overlooked until some catastrophe—natural or man-induced—forces our attention to its worth. But even so, no sooner is the situation remedied than, more often that not, we revert to our old attitude.

The reason for this sort of indifference is undoubtedly attributable to the fact that, except in exceptional circumstances, water has always been considered as a "gift of the gods", as some thing that human beings are as naturally entitled to as the air they breathe. Its supply, however uneven, has always seemed inexhaustible because water has a natural regenerative cycle which, until the present century, was beyond human control or interference—or even proper comprehension. But the trend of social, political and economic evolution, notably in the past 200 years, with an increase of industry, agriculture, technology, and above all, a vertiginous population growth, as led to a dramatic revision of the age-old belief that no demands made by human populations on the natural resources of the planet are in the process of setting in motion vicious circles in the environment from which it is becoming increasingly difficult to extricate ourselves, not only as concerns the present, but far more important, for the future. Thus, the overuse—or abuse—of water resources has started affecting seriously not only the water cycle but the very nature of water in such a way that, in conjunction with other abuses of the environment, the results have been climate changes, droughts, flooding, desertification on the one hand and acid rain, water pollution and eutrophication on the other.

Actually, the problem of water is to be considered less in terms of quantity—though with a steeply increasing world population making increasingly heavier demands on a fixed quantity of water, one will sooner or later be confronted with this aspect of the problem too—than in terms of proper distribution of available resources taking into account sound management, stock age and maintenance of quality. For among the major pre-occupations of humanity in the coming years, adequate supply of freshwater to the teeming populations figures in the forefront. Between 1900 and 2000 water consumption will have globally increased tenfold and though the share of agriculture, the major consumer of fresh water, is expected to drop significantly (from 90 per cent to 62 per cent approximately), that of industry and the cities will have increased enormously (approximately, from 6 per cent to 24 per cent and 3 per cent to 8 per cent respectively).

Given the current trend of societal evolution i.e. greater emphasis on industry and increasing migration towards the cities added to the global population boom, these figures are certainly cause for concern. Not only because of the damages caused to freshwater resources through the increasing use of fertilizers in the search to maximize agricultural production to cater to the increasing populations, but equally because the mushrooming of industries and urban concentrations are sources of increasing water pollution. Though the industrialised nations have more than their fair share of blame in this matter insofar as the current state of water pollution goes, for the future, it is in the developing world that lies the major source of concern. Lack of resources for adequate urban planning, the increasing role of industry in the search for economic solutions added to uncontrollable population pressures are already on they way to creating an explosive situation in a great number of developing nations with the available water supply becoming more and more inadequate in terms of quantity as well as quality. And then one considers the fact that around 80 per cent of all diseases are estimated to be water related, and that by the year 2000, 51 per cent of the world population will be urban based, one can hardly be accused of exaggeration in speaking of an explosive situation.

Attacking such a vast problem is no mean task. Water being at the very source of life, what concerns water concerns every aspect of life. Thus, be it climate change, pollution, desertification, deforestation, food production....or whatever other major environmental problem that humanity is confronted with today, water constitutes one of the prime factors. Managing our water resources with care and intelligence for the use of present and future generations is a major responsibility which has to be shared by governments and the public alike, for no sector alone can deal efficiently with so vital a problem which affects not only the present but also the future of humanity. Again, as in the case of biodiversity and climate change, the problem of water being a global problem, international cooperation is of utmost importance since activities in one part of the planet are likely to produce consequences in other regions of the world.

Concerted action by the international community alone is capable of dealing effectively with a problem of such far-reaching consequences.

If our planet is to be saved from disaster—for in jeopardising our water resources we are guilty of nothing less than condemning life itself on our planet—we have to work for sustainable results: short-term plans for the present which will dovetail into medium-term ones for the coming generations without compromising the possibility, at the same time, of careful long-term planning to guarantee the future of the planet. In this, the part of environmental education and information of the people is fundamental. No strategy, no policy, no plan—be it ever so well prepared and implemented—can hope to succeed without the active and effective participation of the main actors—the people who must be properly educated and informed. For this age-old techniques, beliefs—mentalities must be brought in line with present day realities. People have to learn to think differently in order to veer from a course which, however right in the past, has been shown to be less than adequate for present conditions—and catastrophic for the future—and must therefore needs be altered.

Changing mentalities is neither an easy nor a rapid process. It is difficult to go back upon the accumulated experience of generations—even in the face of stark realities and scientific evidence. Moreover, when dealing with such global and fundamental issues as water, where even "scientific evidence" tends to be stated in tentative terms, the task becomes more onerous. Add to this the fact that the problem presents itself most presently in developing countries which are equally subject to enormous economic pressures which tend to reduce the cope of possible solutions. We are thus faced with the enormous task of trying to change attitudes, values, mentalities of populations whose geographical, socio-cultural and economic conditions have already fashioned priorities other than those that would precisely permit them to overcome their difficulties in a sustainable manner. In other words, of persuading people of abandon traditional short-term strategies in favour of perhaps more unattractive but eventually sustainable, long-term practices.

A veritable Herculean labour—which can only be accomplished through information and education. And in particular, through environmental education and information whose avowed aim is precisely to develop the understanding, knowledge, skills and motivations leading to the acquisition of attitudes, values and mentalities which are necessary to deal effectively with environmental issues and problems. Sound and systematic environmental education of the people associated with concerted local, national and international action, is the only means to finding a sustainable solution to this problem. The ground has to be paved through adequate information on the subject followed by educative processes adapted to specific local conditions. For a uniform education, whether formal or non-formal, might perhaps do more harm than good as its rejection, due to its unsuitability in the light of local customs, beliefs, traditions... might only serve to reinforce the very attitudes that it seeks to change. In each region, each country, each locality the educative processes must correspond to the socio-cultural, historical, economic conditions of the people. Only then can we hope to arrive at the change in mentalities around the planet which, coupled with consistent, parallel support from national and international institutions, will lead to the safeguard of what is perhaps our most precious resource—Water.

28

Consumption Bomb

It is three decades since we passed the peak world population growth rate of 2.04 per cent. Annual additions too are now a decade past their peak of 86 million a year. They are currently running at 78 million a year and are heading downwards. A peak in total numbers, however, still lies at least four or five decades ahead. On the UN Population Division's 1998 projections, the total is likely to reach 8.9 billion in 2050. The long range medium projection, which has not been updated since 1996, expects world population to level out at just under 11 billion in 2200 AD.

However, this is based on assumptions that are increasingly questionable. More and more countries are reaching levels of female fertility that are not enough for replacement—below 2.1 children over the lifetime of each women. At the latest count there are 61 countries in this category. Of this 23 had very low fertility, below 1.5.

The situation is unprecedented in times of global peace on economic growth. The UN medium projection assumes that where fertility is very low it will rise again to 1.7-1.9 children per woman. In all countries where fertility is currently above replacement level of 2.1, it assumes that it will not fall below that level.

Yet fertility has fallen below replacement level in so many countries, which such different cultures and different stages of economic growth, that is increasingly looking as if low fertility may be here to stay. If this became the case, then world population may peak at some where between 8 and 9 billion. Thereafter it may well begin to decline. The 1996 long range low projection has world population falling to 5.6 billion in 2100 AD.

None of this means that reproductive rights should have lower priority in future. Their contribution to the health and welfare of women and children are clear. Many poor countries in Africa and South Asia face huge population increases which will be hard to accommodate without major problems of land and water scarcity. In these areas reproductive rights receive a very high priority.

Increasingly our concern must focus on consumption, and how we can cope with the effects of its inexorable increase. Over the past 25 years world population increased by 53 per cent, but world consumption per person (Measured by income) by only 39 per cent. Assume that consumption per person will rise 100 per cent, while population will rise by only half that amount. As time goes on the preponderance of consumption will increase more and more.

There is a crucial difference between population and consumption aspirations. If fully assured of children's survival most people have quite modest desire for family size. But their desire to consume knows no upper bounds. As wealth increases, people double-up their possessions; two or three cars, two bathrooms, two rooms with all contents, two or three holidays a year.

Appliances improve every year and old ones "need" replacing. New needs are created that never existed before. Globalisation is making products cheaper than ever. TVs are no longer uncommon even in African shanty towns. The number of households is increasing as people live longer and family breakdown becomes more common. Smaller households consume considerably more per per cent than large. Moreover, consumption is politically very difficult to restrain. No one can get elected promising people they can earn and spend less, or re-elected if they fulfil their promises.

In view of this much of the burden of reducing our environmental impact will rest on technology. Technology will have to deliver major shifts in improving resource productivity, and in reducing the amount of waste we create. All our institutions and forms of management which affect technology will need to be geared to this end.

In some areas the record has been good and looks likely to remain so. Productivity has kept up with demand in the case of resources that are traded on markets, and that are under the direct control of people or companies affected by shortages or prices. Global food production has kept pace with demand: although land and cereal production per person has declined, average intakes of calories and protein have continued to improve and are at record levels. Malnutrition persists, but this is due to poverty and landlessness, not to the inability of the world to produce enough food. We have not encountered any limiting shortage of any key mineral resources or of energy. Nor are we likely to, because we continually economise and find substitutes, there has been a gradual reduction in the material used for each unit of production.

The prospects are much worse for resources that are not traded on markets or subject to sustainable management, as yet. These include groundwater, state forests, ocean fish, biodiversity in general. They include communal waste sinks like rivers, lakes and oceans, and the global atmosphere. In all of these areas it looks likely that things will get quite a lot worse before they get better.

These kinds of resources and sinks are not under the direct control of people affected by shortage or damage. People wishing to change the way a common resource or sink is used or managed have to pass through the legal or political system. They must organise, take out lawsuits against polluters, pressurise legislators and so on. Political responses are typically slow. Usually the majority of voters have to be convinced of the need for action before politicians will risk taking action. Even then powerful and rich vested interest will lobby hard for the status quo, and will often succeed in frustrating changes that are desired by a global majority. America's coal, oil, and car lobbies have stood in the way of any significant US commitment to reduce carbon dioxide output, and the US is the world's largest emitter of carbon dioxide.

Usually there has to be very widespread and very visible environmental damage before action is taken. The thinning of the ozone layer fitted that category well and the response was swift. North Atlantic fishing reached that point in the 1990s, yet politicians shied away from taking adequate action until the last moment: fishing stocks plummeted and there was massive job loss. Global warming is still long way from the damage being widespread enough, and attributable clearly enough to human activities, for politicians to be ready to speed up the move into renewable energy.

The question with the common resources and sinks is always: will we react in time? The answer is all the more difficult because we usually don't know in advance what is "in time." Many critical changes are subject to threshold effects. When a certain point is crossed, very sudden and disastrous change can occur with little warning. In many cases we do not know where the thresholds lie.

Prudence dictates a preventive approach—a stitch in time saves nine. But the history of environmental problems shows that politicians rarely act decisively until the brink is reached, and it will always be touch and go whether we are pushed over it or not.

* * * *

29

Government Intervention and Private Enterprise

Poverty reduction is impossible if the economy does not flourish, driven by a dynamic private sector. However, a purely market-led strategy simply increases corporate profits. It does not help a national economy to develop. Japan and the East Asian "tiger states" took a different approach. In these cases, strong governments competently directed private enterprise. Development policy should consider this model.

Cashewnuts are a popular snack with an evening beer but, far more importantly, they are a major economic asset for a number of African countries. Tanzania and Guinea-Biassau each account (or accounted) for 8 per cent of world production. Ivory Coast for six per cent and Mozambique for three percent. The importance of cashew nuts is even clearer if looked at from the countries perspective. They were Mozambique's second largest export product for a long time-next to sugar. Today, however, most of the factories which processed cashewnuts for export have closed down in Mozambique and Tanzania. This has been caused by the privatisation and liberalisation policy of the World Bank and the International Monetary Fund. What happened?

Mozambique had built up an industry processing cashewnuts for export. In 1994-95, at the insistence of the World Bank, the 18 state-owned businesses, with approximately 10,000 employees, were privatised and passed into the hands of local business people. No sooner had this happened, than the World Bank released a study which claimed that the processing industry was so inefficient that the country was losing money. The bank said it would be more profitable to export raw nuts to India: the country's export earnings would increase, as would farmer's incomes. Until then, Mozambique's government had banned the export of unprocessed nuts in order to protect its own industry. The multilateral organisations now made the free export of cashews a strict condition for further loans and the government found itself forced to lift the ban.

As a result, most of the businesses had to cease production (in 2005, only seven of the 18 were still in operation). Nonetheless, farmers did not make any more money than before. Middlemen were pocketing the profit, factory workers were on the streets and export earnings dropped. Whereas Mozambique earned $151 million in 1971 from cashew exports, the figure had gone down to only $11.5 million by 2005.

In a study carried out subsequently at the personal request of World Bank President James Wolfensohn, then Bank stated that the policy imposed on Mozambique was totally wrong and should be abandoned. It said that the Indian cashewnut industry was only profitable thanks to states subsidies and that, in Mozambique, the value added by processing was a reason to keep the industry alive. It had, however, already been ruined. The latest development was that two transnational corporations (OLAM from Singapore and Technoserve, a US based organisation) formed a partnership in February 2005 to revive the cashew industry in four African countries (including Mozambique). OLAM is the world's largest processor of cashewnuts and also controls the Indian market and Technoserve has the latest technology. Multinationals are taking over.

Serving Corporate Interests

Perhaps it was a mere coincidence that OLAM and Technoserve appeared on the scene. However, an explanation might also be found in a book which appeared on the *New*

York Times 2004 bestseller list "Confessions of an Economic Hit Man" by John Perkins. The author describes how he travelled all over the world, commisioner by the US government and multinationals, to draw the governments of third world countries into a network of US interests, to make them financially dependent and bring them under political and economic control. Perkins describes cases similar to the one above, and others such as that of the Iranian Prime Minister, Mossadegh, who nationalised the American Oil Companies and was thereupon ousted from office. Companies such as Bechtel and Halliburton are named, which recently played disreputable roles in Iraq. These cases are always about restricting the opportunities for autonomous national economic decisions and making the third world countries dependent on the US.

The following case (not one of Perkin's) is another such example. Ghana has some of the world's largest bauxite reserves. After Ghana's independence in 1957, one of President Nkrumah's top goals was to exploit these reserves. Four things were needed: mining the bauxite, an aluminium smelter, sufficient production of electricity and a port. The country funded construction of the port—the colonial government had handed over healthy coffers. The Volta Dam, which allowed cheap electricity to be produced, was financed by an American loan (after Nkrumah had threatened to ask the soviet Union for funds). An amerian consortium, Kaiser/Reynolds, built the aluminium smelter VALCO. This left the most important thing: the bauxite mine. But it was made clear to Nkrumah that this could not be financed too. A contract provide that alumina (the intermediate product between bauxite ore and aluminium) should be imported for ten years—from far-off Jamaica. After ten years, this would be reconsidered.

The Volta Dam delivered the first electricity in 1965, aluminium production began in 1966, Nkrumah as ousted in a coup on in 1967. There are still rumours that the US was involved. The bauxite reserves in Kibi, which is barely

100 km from the port of Tema, were never mined and the contract was still in force until recently. Since there was no duty on the alumina imported and the aluminium exported, Ghana never really reaped any benefits from the project. VALCO was sold by Kaiser to Ghana in 2004. The plant no longer yielded adequate profit with increased cost of electricity. Bauxite mining is now once again under discussion.

The two examples of the cashewnut industry in Mozambique and the aluminium smelter in Ghana clearly show the blessings associated with private enterprise—for internationally active corporations, not for the countries concerned. In both cases, governments were not strong enough to protect the interests of their national economies from the large corporations and other strategic allies. This is one version of how private enterprise development can take place.

Active Governments in East Asia

There is another version which is typical of the East Asian tiger states. It first occurred in Japan and then, following the example, in South Korea and Taiwan, finally in Malaysia and Thailand too. These countries have developed their economies, raised the standard of living for their people and all but eliminated poverty. They did adopt the private, capitalist model for development, but not the market-led-variety. The state kept the leading role for itself. This should not be confused with the state-owned economy found in socialist countries. Here, we are dealing with the model of private enterprise directed by the state.

Japan, an industralised country even before World War II, had to rebuild its economy after 1945. This was done through "administrative guidance" in other words, in close cooperation of government and corporations. The most important state agencies involved were the Ministry of International Trade and Industry (MITI), the Economic Planning Agency (EPA) and the central bank. Special branches in all government bodies ("mirror units") took care of those industries that planners considered most promising. These were targeted by the State for Support and enjoyed preferential credits, subsidised import of machine tools, upgrading of infrastructure, grants for joint research projects and the protection from excessive competition. The Japanese market was shielded from imports for a considerable time, until its own industry was competitive and able to export. This strategy was so effective that Japan soon became an efficient competitor of the old industralised countries.

Development in the "small tiger states" did not follow the Japanese model in all details, but there were more similarities than differences. State control was more rigorous in South Korea (a development dictatorship) than it was in Japan—but the instruments used were similar. The main players in economic development were the large private conglomerates, or "Chaebol", which are similar to the "Keiretsu" in Japan (a set of companies with interlocking business relationships and shareholdings). Apart from state planning specifications, these conglomerates were closely connected to the state by recruiting civil servants as their senior staff. In Taiwan, there were more state owned industries to start with (they clocked up 50 per cent of all industrial value added in 1952). Even in the 1970s and 1980s, state-owned companies were still being set up in industries with high investment costs (steel, ship building, the automotive industry). Only later were they privatised. But as early as the 1960s, there also was rapid growth in small and medium sised enterprises. Their share of exports amounted to 65 per cent in 1988. In both countries, there was a land reform early on, which set the basis for an equitable distribution of wealth and, at the same time, made available the funds for the industrial development.

A second generation of tiger states, Malaysia, Thailand and Indonesia, followed this model with some variations. Malaysia's longstanding Prime Minister Mahathir, designing a Look-East Polilcy, explicity deviated from the European-

American model. The Pioneer Industries Ordinance of 1958 set the direction and was later replaced by the Investment Incentives Act. The other countries had similar laws.

In all these cases, it was decisive that there was (to varying degrees) a "rational bureaucracy" (as defined by Max Weber) which did not merely look at the country with predators eyes. To be sure, there was and is corruption. However, bureaucrats were always well aware that one must first invest before one can reap benefits. Following the model of MITI and EPA in Japan, state planning agencies were set up, which gave the political specifications for economic development: the Economic Planning Board in Korea, the Council for Economic Planning and Development in Taiwan, the Economic Planning Unit in Malaysia, the National Economic and Social Development Board in Thailand. The intellectual elites of the civil service were gathered this way. They followed external advice only if that served the country. Foreign investment (in principle welcome by all means) was subject to strict conditions.

Oskar Weggel, a Hamburg-based Asia expert, confirms that this policy was good for the people of those countries, saying that, astonishingly, growth did not distort the distribution of incomes but, on the contrary, led to a fair distribution which is almost unique worldwide. In the meantime, as the third generation, Mainland China and Vietnam are following the model. They have not yet reached the same stage of development.

Lessons for Poor Countries

The East Asian countries are the only countries in the world to have reached a level of economic and social development similar to Europe and its derivatives in North America and Australia. Neither real socialism in East Europe nor anarchic capitalism in Lain America led to comparable results. Therefore, the question arises what conclusions can be drawn from the Asian experiences for other poor countries in the world. I believe that government-coordinated private enterprise, rather than market liberalism, is the model which national economies should follow if they are to prosoper.

There can no longer be any doubt that the Washington Consensus has failed. However, its successor, the Post-Washington Consensus, only has a vague orientation towards poverty eradication. Nobody has a precise idea what instruments might serve effective implementation. In its justification of a research project called "Operationalising pro-poor growth", the KfW development bank states: "Currently, our knowledge is limited concerning which political measures have to be taken in order to increase the broad-scale impact of economic growth processes." Hopes are mainly directed at an increase in development aid, which could then be used to expand the social sector. There is almost no mention of economic development in the Poverty Reduction Strategy papers, the most important achievement in recent anti-poverty policy. And this while nobody doubts that economic growth is an necessary requirement for poverty reduction.

The creation of an "enabling environment" is still the last word on how to stimulate economic development. However, it has for long been obvious that, on its own, this strategy only leads to cherry-picking by local and foreign investors. They look for individual investment options that are profitable (such as aluminium in Ghana). However, this does not contribute to the development of the national economy, but only serves shareholder interests.

The early development economists in the 1950s and 1960s such as Hirschman, Nurkse and Rosenstein-Rodan, were right after all. Hirsahman expected impulses for development from his concept of "forward and backward linkages", through processinig chains in other words. Rosenstein Rodan recommended the "big push", simultaneously supporting several industries. The names of these development theorists have wronlgy been forgotten. Paul Krugman, one of the most celebrated economists today, called this approach "high development theory" in 1994 and stated that it "really does make a lot of sense, after all".

If development policy is truly interested in starting the economic development of third world countries in corporation with private partners, then it should endeavour to learn from the East-Asian model in some or at least one of its priority countries. This would require first, support for the creation of a planning Board. A number of well-trained and motivated planners and economists originating from the country in question should be recalled from wherever they are currently employed (Europe, USA, international organisations) and be paid attractive salaries. Their task would then be to design an economic and social master plan which should amount to more than a mere wish list. Finally, adequate funds would have to be made available to implement the plan among other things, to draw private investors into the country with appropriate tax and other incentives (but not by providing rent-opportunities).

30

Rural Poverty in India and Development as a Policy Challenge

Poverty can be overcome, and that the poor can increase their income and production within an appropriate framework. Part of that framework is made up of a flow of resources and local-level institutional development, and there is considerable scope for improvement in both. However, the impact of investment and organisation is strictly determined by the nature of the policy environment. While project and programmes can bring some relief to the rural poor, substantial change needs a strong policy commitment. While the poor can overcome poverty, they will not be able to until this becomes a major focus of national policy and action. In the main, this sort of commitment has not been made in the past—at the expense of both the poor and overall development in many areas.

The current state of India is highly contradictory. On the one hand, there is proclamation of a new order; on the other, increasing value is given to sectional and short-term national and group interests. With an overt concern with the India's poor goes an equal weight given to concern with economic mechanisms and relations that pay little attention to poverty and foster more inequality. The dangers of this situation are real. The lack of concrete attention being given to change will mean greater economic polarisation. Greater polarisation among the better-off, and between the better-off and the poor—means instability and a lack of consensus, a lack of legitimacy.

Poverty is far-reaching, and ought to be curtailed. In a period in which resources everywhere appear restricted, this seems not to be an attractive proposition at the practical level. Welfare is everywhere giving way to production as an imperative, just as public expenditure is giving way to private accumulation. Poverty alleviation does not appear to be an idea whose time has come. The objections are great, but they are also misplaced. Poverty alleviation is not necessarily a drain upon accumulation, and it is not primarily a public activity. Poverty alleviation is primarily the activity of the poor themselves, and their progress necessarily involves productive expansion. If this potential for private expansion has not been realised, it is not because of the nature of the poor, it is because of the way in which national economic affairs have been organised. Economic policy has been oriented towards the better off—not infrequently at the expense of the poor. Given the historic association between wealth and power, the definition of development in terms of the large and the wealthy is hardly surprising.

There is the possibility of associated growth involving both large-scale and small-scale production, the better of and the poor. The realisation of this possibility might result from a new social compact. This social compact is not a commitment to social safety nets and welfare, both of which seem to presuppose that the poor are somehow necessarily out of the growth field. It is a commitment to abolishing artificial and onerous terms of exchange that discriminate against the poor, to investing resources where there are real opportunities for gain, irrespective of whether the economic agents concerned are rich or poor, and to creating the space for the poor to organise to pursue their social and economic interests.

There is a need for a new growth model consistent with new social realities. While the 1980s was a period of clearing away many of the obstacles to development, it was not a period in which there emerged a clear vision of what represented the positive basis for growth, beyond, that is, a general prescription of market-driven operations. The model must pass from admonition to positive prescription to fuel growth by integrating the poor in their rightful place in the production function. It must redefine the position of public expenditure in the development process, and seek to establish market structures which are both equitable and open to the participation of the economically weaker elements of the population. Most of all it must revalue the position and contribution of the poor and small-scale producers in the growth process, particularly in the agricultural sector, but not exclusively agriculture.

This means that the issue is not so much one of less government, but of government, both national and local, finding a new rationale for action, including, *inter alia*, creating conditions that will effectively unleash the productive potential of the rural poor.

Financial flows to the poorest Indians are not likely to undergo a very major expansion, especially through private channels. Development will rely very much on the mobilisation of their own resources, and many of these resources are in the hands of the poor, are, indeed, not only the human capital embodied in the poor but also their assets which, while small, individually are cumulatively important in India. The growth model for the 1990s will have to embrace that fact, and build upon it. The paradox of most development models is that they have emphasised the value of what Indians do not have, while devaluing what they have: capital intensity has been promoted in situations of scarcity of capital, at the expense of abundant labour and of low-cost methods of manifold increase of the productivity of assets of which the poor do dispose. In a not very indiret way, the creation of poverty has been subsidised. Poverty alleviation is neither a special topic nor a low-cost substitute for growth. It is neither more nor less "social" than development in general. It is part of the formulation of any sustainable strategy of economic development. In the 1990s it may, and perhaps should, become the dominant issue—not as an alternative to the structural reorganisations of the 1980s, but as a means of filling a growth framework with substance.

31

Crime or Development

Cutting Crime Rates is Essential for Sustainable Development

Crime is increasing almost everywhere in the world. The cost of crime prevention and criminal justice is crippling for many developing countries. Crime scares away investors and undermines the confidence of the people in the organs of the state. But to effectively control crime, social and economic conditions must improve.

Freedom from crime, safety from violence at home and on the street, public safety and the means to make cities safer are essential ingredients of sustainable development. To feel safe from crime is as important to a person as access to food, shelter, education and health.

Available data suggest that crime is increasing all over the world. Robbery, burglary and other interpersonal crimes are believed to have doubled or tripled in industralised countries over the past 30 years. In many other countries, rapid economic and political transition has been associated with a similar escalation of crime rates in a single decade. Urban areas are the worst affected: today, more than half the world's population living in cities of more than 100,000 people are victims of a crime at least once every five years. As more and more of the world's people leave the countryside for the city, crime rates seem locked into an inexorable upward spiral.

The level and type of crime are the result of a range of local, national and regional factors, including traditional culture and belief, political and economic stability, the quality of policing, and the availability of guns and other weapons. In Sao Paolo, for example, a major contributor to the 2,000 annual homicides in the early 1990s was the killing of more than 1,000 suspects per year by the police itself. In the Indian state of Maharashtra, and in Bangladesh, bride-burning and wife-murders account for many of the large number of homicides.

Fear and Reality

But perception of crime may be out of proportion with reality. People commonly believe their society is more violent today than ever before. However, many countries of the North were more violent during the early years of industralisation. Increasing fear of crime, therefore, is not linked in any simple way to growth in actual levels of crime and frequently continues to increase even when crime rates themselves decline. Analysts believe that this accelerating fear of crime is fuelled by ever-faster global communications and greater exposure of crime in the media. The wide-spread perception that crime is out of control can be just as damaging to a country's ability to attract investment as actual levels of crime. Social and political stability are further casualities.

Crime and Development

Development has to be delivered to eliminate the socio-economic triggers of violence; but the delivery itself often triggers violence. However, it is not clear whether development is directly or indirectly linked to crime. Does the development process itself trigger crime, or should the blame fall on the inequality that development often brings about? Many argue that it is the very lack of development that causes crime. There is current research to support either position.

It seems to be certain, though, that urbanisation, rapid liberalisation of the economy, political upheavel, violent conflict and inadequate policing are among the many and complex factors—often linked to poverty and inequality - contributing to growing levels of crime.

The mushrooming growth of cities is a global phenomenon. Urbanisation uproots and dislocates communities and creates new inequalities between haves and have-nots. At the same time, traditional value systems and structures that once served to restrict criminal behaviour are undermined. People become isolated, alienated and less constrained by social norms. As the rural populations of Asia, Latin America and Africa pour into the cities, semi-legal shanty towns appear and grow to accommodate them. Life for hundred of millions of rural migrants means no security of tenure, and little or no work and illegality can soon become their only option.

Cities in the South also have a predominantly young population especially young men—who are every where the main perpetrators of crime. Violent conflict as in many Third World countries is another factor leading to an explosion of crime. It uproots and destroys communities, deprives people of their livelihoods, take young men away from their families and habituates them to violence, rape and killing. Perhaps above all, it saturates a society with guns.

Structural adjustment programmes of World Bank in developing countries which have led to increasing unemployment and cuts of government spending on education and health programmes, have also contributed to rising crime levels. Liberalisation of trade, increased foreign investments, and a rise in international tourism have led to city streets full of expensive foreign cars and shops full of imported luxury goods—a provocative slight for those marginalised by such reforms. Satellite TV which brings the lure of the affluent society even into the shanty towns of the poor is seen as another factor promoting crime and lawlessness.

As governments that have tried to "crackdown on crime" have discovered raising the level of policing alone seldom produces the desired reduction in crime rates. A sustained reduction is more likely to result from a policing strategy that addresses the underlying causes of lawlessness, rooted in urban deprivation and inequality. Nevertheless, public confidence in the police and their effectiveness is acting against crime rates. An effective police force is large, adequately paid and highly trained, ideals that are beyond the reach of many cities of the South. As a result, the police is corrupt in many countries. For instance, government estimates suggest that 70 per cent or more of all police personnel are involved in some form of corruption, ranging from bribetaking to cocaine-trafficking. They derive a significant proportion of their income by extortion from motorists. Many of the problems of corruption can be linked to low pay, low morale and lack of trust in the police force.

The Cost of Crime

Although crime rates are high and increasing worldwide, the cost is disproportionally crippling to countries of the South. Fighting crime can impose a terrible drain on the financial resources of the poorer countries. The global economic cost of urban violence amounts to trillions of US dollars. Crime does not only victimse the individual, but can also destroy communities, ruin businesses and empty state coffers. In the United States alone, the cost of urban crime in 1993 was estimated at $425 billion. In South Africa, the cost of crime was more than $7 billion or 18 per cent of the national budget for 1996/97. Crime and violence are draining resources from families, households, business and government. These costs are completely unsustainable in a developing economy.

High levels of crime scare away foreign tourists and are discouraging both foreign investment and development aid. Crime nurtures an atmosphere of violence, social insecurity and economic stability and deters companies, governments and aid agencies alike. Companies that do set up in cities with high crime rates have to budget specially for the potential cost of theft or damage, or the need to hire extra protection against them. They also have to pay premium salaries to their foreign staff to compensate them for 'hardship posts'. Often, however, companies rather avoid cities where the lives of their staff is in danger. A high level of corruption also tends to work against foreign investment, because it increases transaction costs. Likewise it contributes to lower aid levels as 'donor fatigue' increases when public money is siphoned away from development projects into private pockets.

Dangers to Democracy

Crime also exacts a political cost. Fear and insecurity from crime prompt demands for swift and ruthless action by law enforcement agencies. Governments may seize the opportunity to strengthen a state's repressive apparatus, eroding civil rights by targeting dissidents or political opponents as well as criminals. Where people have no confidence in the state's ability to protect them from crime, alternative forms of crime control, ranging from private security firms to vigilantes and death squads, can emerge. Even worse, the inability of an elected government to control crime is frequently cited as part of the 'justification' for the military to step in and seize power. All too often, the price paid for high levels of crime includes a tragic diminution of democracy and human rights.

Breaking Crime's Stranglehold

Governments, law enforcers, NGOs and development agencies increasingly accept that reducing crime is essential if the countries of the South are to have sustainable development. Criminal justice systems modelled on those of the wealthy countries of the North may be inappropriate for dealing with the problems of developing countries. New forms of cheap, decentralised justice need to promoted, stressing prevention and involving communities. Such systems already exist in some countries.

In the long-term, however, crime prevention is inseparable from social development. Violence and crime are usually the result of inequality and poverty, and they certainly breed fastest in a society characterised by extremes of inequality and social exclusion. Ultimately, only measures that protect communities from deprivation, joblessness, injustice and insecurity will also make them safer from crime.

32

Development
The Third Way

While great claims are being made for the increasingly more efficient and effective technologies perfected to serve development of the people in this scientific age, huge problems are threatening the globe. The problems are mass poverty and hunger, underdevelopment, waste, unemployment, resource scarcity, environmental destruction and armed conflict.

In finding answers to the prevailing problems we must be clear about the meaning and purpose of development. The first glaring mistake made is that development is interpreted as development of the economy and not as the total development of society. When economic development is made the supreme goal, most of the other vital aspects get ignored, namely, development of the political system, community, social cohesion, the ecology, culture and values. Development and stability go hand in hand while poverty and chaos constitute the antithetical twin.

Appropriate Development

The key elements in the conception of appropriate development consist of: first, aiming at sufficiently comfortable material living standards and not affluent standards of the rich as in prosperous nations. Second, development must not be confused with GNP growth. Mere increase of economic activity must not be pursued exclusively at the cost of articles that are urgently needed by the poor majority to maintain them at a reasonable level of material living. Third, in the villages, we must produce articles as are needed by the villagers. Fourth, grassroots and participatory development is essential so that the local people identify and solve their local problems. Fifth, instead of capital and energy intensive high technology, use labour-intensive technology, instead of heavy industrialisation, promote medium scale industries and technologies. And, sixth, instead of preoccupation with a high GNP growth rate, focus on the development of communities and of rural bodies and take care to conserve the local ecosystems. The main purpose should be to meet their primary needs of ordinary people and promotion of their productive resources such as land.

In developing countries like India where billions of poor people remain condemned by conventional economic development strategies and theories, it is vital to introduce appropriate development measures to remove deprivation and ensure the necessity of modest living standards.

The world has witnessed the operation of the two systems namely, the capitalist and the socialist one that have obtained in different countries. Although both the systems have underlined the welfare of all as the basic goal, both have left a legacy of waste, hunger and gross human inequality. Some 1000 million people do not get enough to eat including some 20 million in the USA.

Third World Way of Development

The iniquitous situation in the present day world has sparked off fierce controversies among the conventional economists and the new radical economists who champion a third way, as the alternative way to serve the primary goal of all humanity to have sufficient means to lead a comfortable peaceful life.

In order to achieve prosperity, conventional economists have emphasised the production of bigger cake on the assumption that everyone will get a slice of it. They also argue that a "tide will lift all the boats". Both these assumptions have proved false in that the poor have neither the slice of cake nor has their boat been lifted. Third way system lays stress on highly localised, less cash-reliant and simply structured set-up. It should not be dependent on transport of goods, but concentrate on more local production to meet local needs with a role for barter and free exchange. He urges a radical rethink of conventional economics.

Is this Stepping Backwards?

The most common criticism levelled against the Third Way is that it will arrest the progress made hitherto and that it might mean a return to a 'primitive' way of life. There should be no fear on this score because the Third Way aims at the reduction in the use of resources and therefore, of excessive production and consumption. It does not in any sense mean stepping backwards to a lower level of the quality of life. Nor is the alternative way intended to destroy capitalism or socialism. The conception of the alternate way is to promote economic growth compatible with capitalism and socialism. The ground idea is to promote selflessness, mutual concern and social responsibility. This will replace selfish, competitive and avaricious attitudes as have developed in the conventional economic order of today.

NGO's Resolution at the Rio Conference

That there is increasing awareness of the threat posed by the growing power of multinational corporations was articulated by the international NGO forum in its Declaration resolved on 12 June 1992 at the UN Conference of Environment and Development in Rio de Janerio. The Declaration states that "the Bretton Woods institutions have served the major instruments by which the destruction policies have been imposed on the world" and calls upon "the world's people to protect their economic, social, cultural and environmental interests against the growing power of transnational capital". The Declaration further avers "we recognize the central place of spiritual values and spiritual development... and values of simplicity, love, peace, and reverence for life.

After the failure of the socialist system over four decades to achieve prosperity for all, the Indian Government switched over to the global market economy and is steaming ahead with added liberalisation measures to attract foreign investment and the multinational corporations (MNCs). Some adverse effects of this are already visible: for example, majority financial equity granted to MNCs and the emergence of foreign subsidiaries with cent per cent financial equity; the introduction of pizza and Kentucky Fried Chicken which has been detested by the people in Karnataka. The farmers have also revolted because their rights to produce and sell seeds have been wrested by foreign MNCs who have acquired patent rights over certain Indian crop seeds. In this scenario, the Third Way has much to commend itself to the Government. The Third Way has the air of the Gandhian model of economy and production which emphasizes production by people for their own needs and preference for small and medium sised industry. The same paradigm was championed by the renowned economist Schumacher when he said "Small is beautiful". India should take good care against the present-day headlong drive for the entry of foreign capital and foreign heavy industries.

33

The Population Challenge

During the last half-century world population has more than doubled, climbing from 2.5 billion in 1950 to 5.9 billion in 1998. Those of us born before 1950 are members of the first generation to witness a doubling of world population. Stated otherwise, there has been more growth in population since 1950 than during the 4 million years since our early ancestors first stood upright.

This unprecedented surge in population combined with rising individual consumption, is pushing our claims on the planet beyond its natural limits. Water tables area falling on every continent as demand exceeds the sustainable yield of aquifers. Eventual aquifer depletion will bring irrigation cutbacks and shrinking harvests. Our growing appetite for seafood has pushed oceanic fisheries to their limits and beyond. Collapsing fisheries tell us we can go no further. The earth's temperature is rising, promising changes in climate that we cannot even anticipate. We are triggering the greatest extinction of plant and animal species since the dinosaurs disappeared. As our numbers go up, their numbers go down.

These effects of population growth are relatively recent, but assertions that population growth could affect human welfare are not. In 1798 Thomas Malthus, a British clergyman and intellectual, warned in his famous piece, *An Essay on the Principles of Population,* of the tendency for population to grow exponentially while food supply grew arithmetically. He saw a world where human numbers would continually press against available food supplies.

During the 200 years since Malthus issued his warning, famine has visited countries as diverse as Ireland and India, Ethiopia and China. Indeed, despite the near-tripling of the world grain harvest since 1950 the hungry and malnourished in 1998 number an estimated 840 million—nearly as many people as lived in the world when Malthus penned his essay.

But the nature of famine has changed. Whereas it was once geographically defined by areas of poor harvests, today famine is economically defined by low incomes in those segments of society that lack the purchasing power to buy enough food. Famine concentrated among the poor is less visible than the more traditional version but is no less real.

In addition to checks imposed by food shortages, there is evidence that other checks on population growth are now emerging, such as new infectious diseases, including AIDS, Ethnic conflicts within societies, such as Rwanda and the Sudan, are also taking a growing toll. Water shortages on a scale that would deprive people of enough water to produce food could undermine governments.

The evidence gathered here indicates that the rapid population growth prevailing in a majority of the world's countries is not going to continue much longer. Either countries will get their act together, shifting quickly to smaller families, or death rates will rise from one or more of the stresses just mentioned. As human demands press against more and more of the Earth's limits, the questions is not whether population growth will slow, but how. Will it be because countries do it humanely by shifting quickly to smaller families? Or because they fail to do so, and nature ruthlessly imposes its own constraints? In a world facing many challenges as it prepares to enter the next century, this may be the most challenging of all.

Estimates of future numbers are based on the latest United Nations population projections, using their medium level figures. Under this scenario, world population will grow from 6.1 billion in 2000 to 9.4 billion in 2050—a gain of 3.3 billion. The other two UN projections put global population in 2050 as high as 11.2 billion or as low as 7.7 billion. While the medium scenario is judged by the UN demographers as the one most likely to materialize, it is not an inevitable population part for the next century. Indeed, because the projections are based exclusively on demographic assumptions and do not take into account the environmental limits to carrying capacity, they should be viewed as a first pass rather than the final word on estimates of future population.

We use the medium-level projections to give an idea of the strain this "most likely" outcome would place on ecosystems and governments, and the urgent need to break from the business-as-usual scenario. The mid-level projected growth in population of 3.3 billion by 2050 is very close to the growth that will have occurred between 1950 and 2000, some 3.6 billion. But there is one difference. During the half-century now ending, the growth occurred in both industrial and developing countries. During the next half-century, the entire burden of the projected increase of 3.3 billion will be in developing countries, many of which are hard-pressed to satisfy even existing demands on resources. In fact, the population of the industrial world is expected to decline slightly.

The annual rate of world population growth reached its historical high in 1964 at 2.2 per cent. Since then, it has been slowly declining, dropping to 1.4 per cent in 1998. Despite the falling rate of growth the number of people aged each year increased from 72 million in 1964 to the all-time peak of 87 million in 1990. Since then the annual addition has also declined, falling to 80 million in 1997, where it is projected to remain for the next two decades before starting to decline.

The population projections for individual countries vary more widely than at any time in history. At mid-century populations were growing everywhere, but today they have stabilised in some 32 countries, while they continue to expand in some countries at 3 per cent or more a year. Indeed, the world can be divided demographically into two camps: countries that have achieved population stability or are well on the way to doing so, and those that have not.

With the exception of Japan, all the nations in the first camp are in Europe. And all are industrial countries. The populations of some countries, including Russia, Japan, and Germany, are actually projected to decline some what over the next half-century. In addition to the 32 countries, containing 12 per cent of world population, that have stabilised their populations, in another 39 countries fertility has dropped to replacement level (roughly two children per couple) or below. Among the countries in this category are China and the United States the first and third largest countries, which together contain 26 per cent of the world's people.

Although fertility in these 39 countries has fallen below replacement level, their populations have not yet stabilised because there is a disproportionately large number of young people moving into the reproductive age group. Thus even if they hold their fertility at replacement level, population may continue to grow for several decades before it stabilizes. It was this realisation that led China nearly 20 years ago to shift its goal from a two-child to a one-child family. Leaders in Beijing realised that, if they did not do this they would be faced with adding the equivalent of another India to their population—a development they considered potentially disastrous for their people.

In contrast to this group some countries are projected to triple their populations over the next half-century. For example, Ethiopia's current population of 62 million will more than triple, as it climbs to 213 million in 2050. Pakistan's population is projected to go from 148 million to 357 million, surpassing that of the United States before 2050 today to 339 million, giving it more people in 2050 than there were in all of Africa in 1950. From an environmental Vantage point, considering particularly the availability of water and cropland, it is unlikely that the projected population increases for these three countries, and other countries with similar projected gains, will materialise.

As hard as it is to imagine the additicn of another 3.3 billion people to the world's population, it is even more difficult to understand the effects of adding such numbers. As we look back over the last half-century, we see that World lumber use more than doubled, paper use increased nearly six-fold, grain consumption nearly tripled, water use tripled, and fossil fuel burning increased some four-fold. The relative contribution of population growth and rising affluence to the growth in demand for various resources varies widely. With lumber use, most of the doubled use is accounted for by population growth. With paper, in contrast, rising affluence is primarily responsible for the growth in use.

One way to understand the consequences of future population growth is to contrast some of the key trend projected for the next half-century with those of the as one. For example, we have seen a new five-fold growth in the oceanic fish catch and a doubling in the supply available per person, but biologists now believe we may have "hit the wall" in oceanic fisheries and that the oceans cannot sustain a catch any larger than today's. Thus people born today are likely to see the catch per person cut in half during their lifetimes.

Grainland per person has been shrinking since mid-century, but the drop projected for the next 50 years means the world will have less grainland per person than India has today. Future population growth is likely to reduce this key number in many societies to the point where they will no longer be enable to feed themselves. Countries such as Ethiopia, India, Nigeria, and Pakistan will see grainland per person shrink by 2050 to less than one tenth of a hectare (one fourth of an acre)—far smaller than a typical suburban building lot in the United States.

Given that at the amount of fresh water produced each year is essentially fixed by nature, the water available, per person has shrunk steadily as a result of population growth, leading to sever water shortages in some areas. Countries now experiencing these shortages include China and India, along with scores of smaller ones. As irrigation water is diverted to industrial and residential uses.

The challenge to governments presented by continuing rapid population growth is not limited to natural resources. It also includes education, housing, and jobs. During the last half-century the world has fallen further and further behind in creating jobs, leading to record levels of unemployment and underemployment. Unfortunately over the next 50 years the number of entrants into the job market will be even greater. Few things threaten the political stability of a country as much as growing ranks of unemployed young people.

As noted earlier, the UN population projections cited here are based on exclusively demographic assumptions, which are not related to the population carrying capacity of local eco-systems. These projections are purely statistical, based on historical data on fertility, mortality, and average life span and assumptions about future trends.

Based on the analysis in it, I conclude that the medium projection of 9.4 billion people in 2050 which UN demographers consider to be the most problem is unlikely to materialize. Rather the world is more likely to follow a path closer to the low population projection of 7.7 billion by mid-century.

What is less clear is whether we will move to the lower trajectory because countries with rapid pollution growth quickly shift to smaller families or because they fail to do so and the resulting inability to manage threats from disease, spreading hunger, or social disintegration leads to rising death rates.

* * * *

34

A Rare and Precious Resource

Fresh water is a scarce commodity. Since it's impossible to increase supply, demand and waste must be reduced. But how?

Water is a bond between human beings and nature. It is ever-present in our daily lives and in our imaginations. Since the beginning of time, it has shaped extraordinary social institutions, and access of it has provoked many conflicts.

But most of the world's people, who have never gone short of water, take its availability for granted. Industrialists, farmers and ordinary consumers blithely go on wasting it. These days, though, supplies are diminishing while demand is soaring. Everyone knows that the time has come for attitudes to change.

Few people are aware of the true extent of fresh water scarcity. Many are fooled by the huge expanses of blue that feature on maps of the world. They do not know that 97.5 per cent of the planet's water is salty—and that most of the world's fresh water—the remaining 2.5 per cent—is unusable: 70 per cent of it is frozen in the icecaps of Antarctica and Greenland and almost all the rest exists in the form of soil humidity or in water tables which are too deep to be tapped. In all, barely one per cent of fresh water –0.007 per cent of all the water in the world, is easily accessible.

Over the past century, population growth and human activity have caused this precious resource to dwindle.

Between 1900 and 1995, world demand for water increased more than six fold—compared with a threefold increase in world population. The ratio between the stock of fresh water and world population seems to show that in overall terms there is enough water to go round. But in the most vulnerable regions, an estimated 460 million people (8 per cent of the world's population) are short of water, and another quarter of the planet's inhabitants are heading for the same fate. Experts say that if nothing is done, two-thirds of humanity will suffer from a moderate to severe lack of water by the year 2025.

Inequalities in the availability of water—sometimes even within a single country—are reflected in huge difference in consumption levels.

Scarcity is just one part of the problem. Water quality is also declining alarmingly. In some areas, contamination levels are so high that water can no longer be used even for industrial purposes. There are many reasons for this untreated sewage, chemical waste, fuel leakages, dumped garbage, contamination of soil by chemicals used by farmers. The worldwide extent of such pollution is hard to assess because data are lacking for several countries. But some figures give an idea of the problem. It is thought for example that 90 per cent of waste water in developing countries is released without any kind of treatment.

Things are especially bad in cities, where water demand is exploding. For the first time in human history, there will soon be more people living in cities than in the countryside and so water consumption will continue to increase. Soaring urbanisation will sharpen the rivalary between the different kinds of water users.

Curbing the Explosion in Demand

Today, farming uses 69 per cent of the water consumed in the world, industry 23 per cent and households 8 per cent. In developing countries, agriculture uses as much as 80 per cent. The needs of city-dwellers, industry and tourists are expected to increase rapidly, at least as much as the need to produce more farm products to feed the planet. The problem of increasing water supply has long been seen as a technical one, calling for technical solutions such as building more dams and desalination plants. Wild ideas towing chunks of icebergs from the poles have even been mooted.

But today, technical solutions are reaching their limits, Economic and socio-ecological arguments are levelled against building new dams, for example: dams are costing more and more because the best sites have already been used, and they take millions of people out of their environment and upset ecosystems. As a result, twice as many dams were built on average between 1951 and 1977 than during the past decade.

Hydrologists and engineers have less and less room for manoeuvre, but a new consensus with new actors is taking shape. Since supply can no longer be expanded—or only at prohibitive cost for many countries—the explosion in demand must be curbed along with wasteful practices. An estimated 60 per cent of the water used in irrigation is lost through inefficient systems, for example.

Economists have plunged into the debate on water and made quite a few waves. To obtain "rational use" of water, i.e. avoiding waste and maintaining quality, they say consumers must be made to pay for it. Out of the question, reply those in favour of free water, which some cultures regard as "a gift from heaven". And what about the poor, ask the champions of human rights and the right to water? Other important and prickly questions being asked by decision-makers are how to calculate the "real price" of water and who should organise its sale.

The State as Mediator

The principle of free water is being challenged. For many people, water has become a commodity to be bought and sold. But management of this shared resource cannot be left exclusively to market forces. Many elements of civil society—NGO's, researchers, community' groups—are campaigning for the cultural and social aspects of water management to be taken into account.

Even the World Bank, the main advocate of water privatisation, is cautious on this point. It recognises the value of the partnerships between the public and private sectors which have sprung up in recent years. Only the state seems to be in a position to ensure that practices are fair and to mediate between the parties involved—consumer groups, private firms and public bodies. At any rate, water regulation and management systems need to be based on other than purely financial criteria. If they aren't, hundreds of millions of people will have no access to it.

35

What was Wrong with Structural Adjustment

In Defence of a Much-Maligned Strategy

After decades of stranded development theories, ideologies and paradigms, "structural adjustment", with its demands for clean fiscal policy and an end to uneconomic state enterprises, political privileges, market and exchange rate intervention and corruption, entered the aid arena like a refreshing dawn after a long night of frustrating dreams. Only the "old guard" of planned economy advocates and jealous academicians who had missed the boat were able to shut their eyes to the moral and economic justification of this liberating breakthrough in international development policy spearheaded by the Bretton Woods institutions then steered by some exceptionally courageous economists.

Reaction to SAPs

As with any revolution, defeat is awaiting the pioneers at the hands of political power greed, reactionary tactics by the formerly privileged and academic envy. The principal device serving the reactionary forces as a lever of influence on the mood of the "development community" has been the identification and dramatisation of new pockets or strata of (principally urban) poverty allegedly created by structural adjustment measures, while shunning the much broader-based rise in economic activity, real incomes and sense of fair reward in the overall society, especially the rural population. That the hardship experienced by urban poor, formerly privileged under consumer price control and import subsidies to the debit depressed farm prices or maintained by grossly over-expanded public payrolls, was only laying open the camouflaged erosion of the economy and near-bankruptcy of governments and public enterprises was conveniently downplayed.

These reactionary howls were to be expected. Not that they met the entirely innocent. There had been naively sweeping, overly assuming demands by some structural adjustment missions. But an intellectually vigorous and dynamic "development community" would have coped with the ensuing opposition, strengthened the analytical and monitoring capacities and the political will to endure also rocky roads and bitter medicines on the way to a healthier base. Instead, institutional rivalry, political opportunism and emotive populism were thriving. In a way, the "development community" behaved as if it did not want its patient to become able to stand on his own feet and eventually steal its raison d'être.

Worst, the Bretton Woods institutions themselves, partly under the pressure of the emotive opposition, described above, fell to the temptation to rescue their lending volume, which was threatened by the frugality dictated to Third World public budgets under structural adjustment recipes, through hardship-easing loans. They thereby corrupted their creation in using it to reinforce their indispensability. As a consequence it soon turned out that some of the most obedient loan takers under structural adjustment terms experienced sharply rising indebtedness, exploited as a disqualifying symptom by the anti-structural adjustment camp.

Whatever the opinions on structural adjustment policies, the commitment to the principles of "good governance" has come to stay, at least on paper, as an almost standard conditionally for official development aid from OECD donor countries. The realisation, matured in the implementation of structural adjustment programmes, that not the quantity of aid, but the quality of Third World governments determines the positive or negative course of development, may be regarded as the most valuable fruit of the decades—old policy debate in the 'development community". And the use of aid as a pressure or bribing factor towards "good governance" as foreign aid's least disputable purpose.

Out of the Limelight

Nothing, however, must be taken for granted. Achievement breeds its challenge! Structural adjustment, though in essence hardly disputable has been pushed out of the limelight and replaced by the oldest actor in the company: eradication of poverty, twinned with an equally perpetual endeavour at the macro-level: debt-forgiveness. This falling back to square one in donors' approach to the problems of the south, i.e., the call to alleviate poverty and priorities direct efforts to this end above all other developmental efforts—does it indicate a sell-out of constructive ideas in the "development community"? Has any noteworthy progress been achieved in the past by this approach?

By telling a frugally toiling but independent subsistence farmer that internationally his condition is classed as "poverty", deserving compassion and support by the world community and cancellation of his debts, one can hardly expect a sustainable improvement in his output, satisfaction, or self-respect and even less, when he realises that the help principally provides jobs, fringe benefits and self-importance to a gamut of intermediaries, at home and abroad.

What do those poverty advocates (the "Lords of poverty") really know about the resources, life management, value systems and ambitions of those they generalize by the billions? The great variance in the conception of life situations, from different external viewpoints.

What the aid system can do for these rural populations classed as "poor"/"underprivileged"/"exploited", is press for justice, i.e., "good governance". The achievements of structural adjustment policy through, e.g. abolishing official price and exchange rate distortions, import subsidies and exploitative state agencies, has brought massive income improvement for peasant populations, i.e. the majority of LDC inhabitants, in dimensions unreachable by whatsoever direct "attack" on rural "poverty". What people want is not being benevolently treated as poor, but being justly rewarded for their work, i.e., by access to the unmanipulated market value of their output. Slackening on structural adjustment/"good governance" conditionally under the present "10 year itch" for paradigm change means foregoing much of the potential opportunities for undoing injustice and exploitation of the masses. It should be clear where priority focus should be placed in ODA policy.

Small is not Beautiful

The direct attack on "poverty", orchestrated by the Bretton Woods institutions under their freshly launched Poverty Reduction Strategy Paper (PRSP) campaign, is being rightly regarded as primarily an NGO domain, since most activities are expected to be carried out at local community level. This would require careful screening and coordinating of NGO activities and their integration via gradual expansion of their experience. But "small" is not "beautiful" for the development financing institution. Disbursement needs are pressing, calling for the new paradigm to quickly provide channels for another wave of loans to the "IDA Countries". Their problem of heavy indebtedness, which would principally exclude most of them from any new loan consideration, shall be solved with one stroke (which only the well-cushioned development bureaucracy can afford); debt relief against presentation of country PRSPs by the respective governments. NGOs are expected to play in the system especially the knowledge gap about the "poor" people's real wants and needs NGOs will naturally be tempted by such expansionary boost to their involvement (referred to sarcastically as their philanthropic empire" by an African conference participant), but this will not be conducive to quality and accountability of their performance, which ideally should be based on private sponsorship in combination with strong target-group provided self-help components.

Patience and Self-Restraint

Local knowledge and initiatives cannot be obtained under time pressure. "The grass does not grow faster by being pulled". When will the "development community" learn patience and self-restraint in the approach to LDC's capacity for constructive absorption of aid programmes accompanied by a genuine sense of ownership?

After all these deliberations, how shall development policy be shaped in order to better correspond with reality, without sinking deeper into hypocrisy and frustration?

To come back to the opening question: what was wrong with "structural adjustment"? Nothing was wrong with its intent. In fact this was very right and long overdue. Its implementation, however, lacked patience, perseverance and solid support from the development community, apart from its being corrupted as a vehicle for expansionary lending policy. If aid is meant to not be an end in itself, then structural adjustment policy needs constant reinforcement, underpinned by strict lending discipline. There should be an end to irresponsible lending and easy escape from its consequences by wholesome periodic debt relief burdened on the international tax-paying community. No ODA, either loans or grants, should be made available to governments who are not in active process of implementing "good governance" principles. A monitoring unit, reporting to the donor community on government performance in regard to its "good government"? Structural adjustment commitment, should be maintained in each and receiving country by "donor consortia" comprising all locally represented bilateral and multilateral development organisations currently extending technical, financial or material assistance to the country.

In order to accommodate the poverty focus without diluting the necessary structural adjustment orientation of ODA, a division of activity-focus between the latter and the NGO sector would seem to be advantageous.

- ODA, limited to the countries abiding to structural adjustment/"good governance" conditionally, with focus concentration on sustainable physical, social and economic infrastructure principally at national and regional level, public management training, higher education and research, consultant and senior adviser services.
- The NGO sector, principally funded by private sponsorship, united to structural adjustment conditionally (but preferably grafted on local self-help initiative), with focus-concentration on the Third World "poor", i.e., mostly at rural community and low-income township level, for amelioration of living conditions and local resource utilisation.
- Strengthening of linkages between the NGO sector and the UN Technical Agencies to mutual benefit: NGOs in need of professional information, evaluation and advice or forum for discussion to find an actively supportive window at the agencies; the latter to maintain and develop field contact of research and policy generation, not least as a substitute for their declining project work (giving way to greater concentration on their global functions, i.e., serving as information, policy initiation, and coordination/negotiation centre on topics of global concern, such as e.g., human rights, global monetary and trade systems, tropical forest and global marine resources, global and regional health threats, international standards).

In conclusion, it may be called to mind that aid and its institutions have no claim for permanence. They are justified only as temporary functions in a phasing-out process of self-help support. Any claim for unlimited continuity would breed lasting infantilisation.

****

36

For a Fair Sharing of Time

Women may have entered public life on a massive scale, but they are still on their own when it comes to running the household. A new balance must be struck if there is to be genuine democracy. At the drawn of the 21st century, states and the international community can no longer refute the fact that humanity is made up of two sexes, not just one. This discovery, a precious legacy of the century that just closed, has brought women's existence into the limelight. One of the great democratic challenges for societies over the next century will be to mature so that both sexes are able to live their lives on an equal footing, with all their differences, contrasting history and culture, but also with equal rights and responsibilities.

Women's rise to power and their participation in politics are the vital signs of a healthy democracy. If only this vision that emerged from the 1995 Beijing Women's Conference could spread worldwide! one can call it a radicalisation of democracy. When women take part in the public arena, contributing to the ongoing, shared effort to shape better ways of living together, a qullitative leap occurs. Their participation fills a gap which has until now prevented the emergence of a truly democratic culture.

Archaic Attitudes

But attitudes are not the only obstacle to women's ambitions. The structure of society and the way men and women run their daily lives are other stumbling blocks. The Inter-American Development Bank has had the good idea of giving the Institute for Cultural Action, and NGO in Rio de Janeiro, the task of setting up a pilot programme to train women for positions of political and social power. Participants include trade union and NGO leaders, key figures from the black and indigenous communities, company executives, civil servants and policy-makers.

These women of different ages, educational backgrounds and ethnic origins are all aware of one fact: they are paying a very high price for a social contract that was negotiated when women were in a position of weakness, and agree that this has to change.

Remapping the Division between Public and Private Life

In Rio de Janeiro revealed that there is an urgent need to reorganize the use of time, to strike a new balance between responsibilities and to remap the division between public and private life. Household tasks must be recognised as time consuming, socially and economically vital and a serious check on women's ambitions.

Women in positions of power must constantly prove that they can behave like men. They keep quiet about having to look after children, run a household and care for elderly parents. Bringing those issues out into the open would mean admitting "flaws" that men do not have, for the simple reason that they delegate such work to their wives.

By drawing a veil of silence over their home life as if it were something illicit, women are allowing a basic fact to be hidden: the world of work relies on a domestic zone run by there. Women have changed, but the world of work has not and they are reaching the point of exhaustion. Filled with a deep sense of injustice, they are asking themselves: "Where did I go wrong?"

Understanding that humanity is composed of two different but equal sexes has several implications. Society must redefine itself because women are turning up in public carrying children in their arms and breast-feeding them, and because they have their own awareness and language that come from life experiences which are different from those of men.

An Untenable Double Burden

Articulating issues affecting public and private lifc is complicated, but that does not mean the equation is impossible of that the problems they raise should be brushed aside especially since the two worlds of public and private life are intertwined and mutually supportive. The balance between the two has now been upset. Women have entered public life on a massive scale, but the organisation of home life how time is used and who is responsible for what tasks is still the same, as if nothing had changed. And yet such a world, where women are expected to soldier on just as before, "simply adding to their lives experiences hitherto reserved to men, is called egalitarian.

That misunderstanding is fueled by and age-old tradition of dismissing the world of women, even by women themselves. Because society does not consider what they do in the home as having any major social significance, it fails to add this part of their lives to the other side of the equation.

This is why the massive migration of women from the home to the public arena is occurring without societies having to think seriously about how and by whom domestic work will be done in the future (and which women still do, but at what cost!). The double burden, resulting from an out dated social contract, is putting women under mounting pressure by speeding up their lives to an untenable pace. We are facing a social problem that society as a whole must solve and not, as many think, a problem that women must settle by working even harder.

As new areas of power open up to women, both sexes must take a fresh look at how they use time. Rearranging it is a challenge to society's imagination. But has this necessity sunk into the minds of decision-makers? I do not think so. This poses a major problem because it is a missing building block in the construction of our democracies.

The everyday work is proof of this. Women must put these issues on the political and economic agenda, thereby contributing to a more radical definition of democracy. Feminism's new demand for a different sharing of time also opens a debate that goes beyond the interests of women alone. In the final analysis, time and its constants define the limits of our own lives and the range of choices we make, in accordance with the meaning we give to our own existence.

The equality equation is increasingly complex. It is not enough to wipe out the last traces of discrimination in public life. A new definition of equality will emerge when both sexes start sharing responsibility in the private realm. Otherwise, the issue will be distorted and women will lose all chance of succeeding in public life.

37

Development Requires More Ownership

To achieve lasting economic growth and a substantial reduction in poverty, developing country ownership needs to be successively strengthened. The international debate on what constitutes the right economic policy for development has become considerably more intense in re cent years. Some of the recommendations that prevailed in the 1980s and 1990s, based on neoclassical economic theory, had to be revised. Central to the economic recommendations of the 'old' Washington Consensus were liberalisation and deregulation of the economy as well as 'neutral' monetary and fiscal policies.

With the Cologne debt relief initiative the Washington consensus and its structural adjustment strategy were basically relegated to the past. They were superseded by the concept of Poverty Reduction Strategy Papers (PRSPs). This approach depends on developing countries drafting policies themselves ("ownership") with the involvement of civil society ("participation"). So far, however, the international financial institutions have neither thought to the new concepts through to their conclusion nor placed them in a coherent context. Several conceptual gaps still remain.

It is still largely unclear how forces can be mobilised for growth in developing and transition countries and how their economies might be better shielded against external shocks and instability in the light of current trends, it is feared that many countries will hardly achieve the Millennium Development Goals (MDGs) unless sustainable economic growth is attained and har-nessed to reduce poverty.

This suggests that donors have not adequately implemented the new approaches yet. While the Bretton Woods institutions have introduced sweeping reforms—the World Bank has acknowledge the key role institutions and "governance" play in development and has replaced its purely market based approach in favour if more practical solutions—discrepancies between vision and reality persist on the ground.

Shortcomings of the Washington Consensus

Some of the shortcomings of the old policy recommendations are well-known. They ignored distribution issues, for example, paid little attention to the role of institutions, and assigned only a passive role to macro-economic management. The neoclassical equilibrium model on which the Washington Consensus is based permits analysis of allocation aspects but does not take institutional or socio-economic structures into account. The "Standard Packages" of structural adjustment programmes were usually far less differentiated than the related political recommendations in general. Core elements of the programmes were swift privatisation and liberalisation of capital markets. Deregulation and liberalisation were deemed adequate requirements for optimising resource allocation and paving the way for high growth.

Efficient institutions curb insecurity and thus increase readiness to invest. Long-term maintenance of dynamic growth processes is possible only where there are institutions, which' help boost productivity, guarantee a high degree of stability and reduce vulnerability to external shocks.

Unconventional Approaches

Such findings need to be properly thought through and

translated into action. This means actively helping developing and transition countries to plot their own course. it also follows from the paradigm shift marked by PRSP that donors should accept unconventional policy measures. "Ownership" means donor institutions, should open to alternative economic policy options, including macroeconomic options. Without diversity at concept level it will not be possible to mobilise sources of growth on the requisite scale.

The discussion paper makes a number of general conclusions relating to economic policy. They particularly concern the quality of institutions, regulatory systems and governance and the issue of property rights, which needed to be seen as factors fundamental to all other forces for growth. These issues should systematically be taken into account when economic reforms are drafted. This is especially true for reforms based on liberalisation and privatisation. If necessary, liberalising action should be postponed until the minimal requirements are met in institutional and macroeconomic terms. The question of time frames for reform should also be given serious consideration and not—as is often the case—dismissed as a mere detail of "timing and sequencing".

There is no universal recipe for development. Solutions need to be customised and country-specific. It is important that reforms should be anchored in the political, economic and cultural landscape of the developing country in question and that its financial and administrative capaci ties ought to be taken account of. Feasible reform needs to be given higher priority then ideology. Second-best or even third-best options are generally better than "pure doctrine" if they suit the context of the country.

More attention needs to be paid to the question of dept sustainability Financial transfers and especially Overseas Development Agency (ODA) loans—need to result in more investment and higher productivity. Situations where countries amass unsustainable mountains of debt need to be prevented to reduce susceptibility to external shocks. ODA should take account of individual countries' situations. This calls for more flexible, more adequately tailored financing instrument For MICs, the structure of external debt is also significant: short-term volatile currency transfers are particularly problematical.

Confining Conditionality

To increase long-term growth and to substantially reduce poverty. developing country ownership needs to be successively strengthened. Primary requirements are:

- better use and targeted development of local analytical capacities (for instance through Poverty and social impact Analyses—PSIAs);
- advice by external partners (especially the Bretton Woods institutions) on a wide range of policy options including unconventional policy proposals;
- no taboos concerning marcoeconomic issues; they should be included in the PRSP process; and
- greater confinement of World Bank and IMF programme conditionalities to core areas.

Better safeguards should be provided against external shocks. The lending policy of multilateral and bilateral donors needs to be adjusted to suit the debt sustainability of recipient countries in this context, it is important to (continue to) develop financing facilities, which allow swift assistance in the event of external shocks. At the same time, financing instruments need to be designed to reduce debt-servicing risks. Examples could be govemment bonds with interest payment tied to GDP growth or more flexible arrangement for the servicing of concessionary credit. To eliminate exchange rate risks. More ODA loans should be denominated in local currencies.

The World Bank needs to strengthen its strategies for crisis prevention and, in particular, for dealing with external shocks and managing crises.

More account needs to be taken of macro/micro-level interction. Efficient strategies for promoting economic growth and reducing poverty are possible only where macro and micro-policies are functionally interwoven.

Last but not least, PRSP processes need to be improved and poverty reduction and other development strategies made more explicit. It is a well-known fact that many PRSPs do not adequately define priorities, identify trade-offs between the different goals and measures or signal the budgetary implications of the measures that are planned. In particular, theygenerally fail to make any mention of potential sources of future economic growth, let alone craft strategy for mobilising them. Only when these shortcomings are eliminated can PRSPs become real planning tools.

Bibliography

Anand, R.P., *Legal Regime of Sea Bed and the Developing Countries,* 1975.

Bhatt, S., *Environment Protection and International Law,* Radiant Publication, Kalkaji, New Delhi, 1985, p. 122.

Bhatt, S., *Environmental Laws and Water Resources Management,* Radiant Publication, India, and Advent Books Inc., New York, 1986, p. 355.

Behrman, Danial, *In Partnership with Nature—UNESCO and the Environment,* Paris, 1973.

Bell, Daniel, "Technology, Nature and Society", *American Scholar,* Summer, 1973.

Bentley, Glass, Biology and Human Values, USIS, New Delhi.

Book of Nature. The Way Things Work, George Allen and Unwin Ltd., 1981, p. 525.

Boulding, Kenneth E., New Goals for Society, S.H. Schun, ed., *Energy, Economic Growth and the Environment.*

Carr, E.H., *What is History,* 1961.

Darlington, C.D., *The Evolution of Man and Society,* London, 1961.

Downing, Paul B., ed., *Air Pollution and Social Sciences,* New York, 1971.

"Drive to Adopt National Water Policy", *Times of India,* 22 July 1983.

Dubos, Rene, "Man and His Environment", *Britannica Perspectives,* Vol. 1, 1968.

Einstein, A., *My Views,* ed., by S.K. Bandopadhyaya, Calcutta, 1976.

Environment Research Programme, Prepared by NCEPC, Department of Science and Technology, New Delhi.

Forbes, R.J., "The Conquest of Nature and Its Consequences", *Britannica Perspectives,* Vol. 1, 1968.

Fowler, John M., *Energy and Environment,* New York, 1975.

Fuller, Buckminister, R., *Operating Manual for Spaceship Earth,* New York, 1969.

Gandhi, Indira, "Poverty Greatest Pollution, says Mrs. Gandhi", *Times of India,* 8 September 1981.

Glenn, Seaborg, "Science, Technology and Development: A New World Outlook", USIS, New Delhi.

Hacoley, Amos H., *Human Ecology,* New York, 1950.

"India Must Develop Own Ecology", *Times of India,* 8 October 1981.

Marion, Jerry B., *Energy in Perspective,* London, 1974.

Misra, K.C., *Manual of Plant Ecology,* New Delhi, 1980.

Mukherji, P.K., *Life of Tagore,* translate, by S.K. Ghosh, 1975.

Mumford, Lewis, "The Future of Cities", in *Basic Issues in Environment,* E.J. Winn, ed., 1972.

Palmslierna, H., *Future Imperatives for Human Environment,* 1972.

Pavithran, A.K., "World Futurology", *Eastern Journal of International Law,* Madras, Vol. 9.

"Plans to Usher India into 21st Century", *Times of India,* 24 October 1985.

Polunin, Nicholas, "The Biosphere Today", *The Environmental Future,* Proceedings of 1st International Conference on Environmental Future in Finland, ed. by N. Polunin, 1972.

Radhakrishnan, S., *Recovery of Faith,* 1967.

Report on the State of Environment, prepared by Centre for Science and Environment, New Delhi, 1985.

Sarkar, Mahendra Nath, *The Cultural Heritage of India,* Vol. 1.

Sen, Sudhir, "Blueprint for a Better World", *Times of India,* 2 March 1980.

The Limits to Growth, A Report to Club of Rome, New York, 1972.

The Mind of J. Krishnamurti, ed. by L.S.R. Vas, Bombay, 1971.

Toynbee, Arnold, "Man and His Soul", *Hindustan Times,* 4 January 1968.

United Nations List of National Parks and Protected Areas, 1985.

Vivekananda, Swami, *Complete Works,* Vol. II, Calcutta, 1968.

Ward, Barbara and Dubos Rene, *Only One Earth: The Care and Maintenance of a Small Planet,* Report to UN Conference on Human Environment, Stockholm, 1972.

"Wildlife Laws in India", *Times of India,* 4 March 1985.

Ward, Barbara, *Progress for a Small Planet,* 1979.

Index

❑❑❑